The
WILD WEST
CATALOG

BRUCE WEXLER

Skyhorse Publishing

CONTENTS

The Cowboy 8

The Chuckwagon 30

Native Americans in the West 44

Native American Artifacts 54

The US Cavalry 60

Fort Smith 80

Gunfighters of the Old West 96

Guns of the Wild West 114

Western Characters 132

Women in the West 156

The Grandest Enterprise Under God 174

Western Towns 186

Sodbusters, Logcabins, and Frames 198

Boomers, Sooners, and Moonshiners 204

The Old West in Popular Culture 212

Western Toys 238

THE MAGNIFICENT WEST

While America without the West is now unthinkable, its assimilation into the nation was an epic achievement. A tremendous feat, which took over a century. The story of the West is the story of every settler that made it to the region, even those that left empty-handed. It is the story of countless individualists that went West to live their own lives: farmers, preachers, tarts, ladies, businessmen, gunslingers, cowboys, miners, medicine men, gamblers, trappers, and all the rest. The story of the West is a fantastic drama with any number of players.

Without a doubt, the most fascinating period in Western history is the century between 1800 and 1900. This was an era of the most fundamental change, when the West evolved from an untamed landscape to become part of the modern world. Packed with an infinite variety of human experience, this century left a huge impression on the region. As well as mass migration, this century also saw the indissoluble linking of Atlantic and Pacific coasts. Connected in turn by the pioneer trail, stagecoach, Pony Express, railroad, and telegraph, a single nation was gradually forged.

With equal certainly, we can also acknowledge that this century was also the most complex in the region's history. As well as bravery, ingenuity, and fortitude, it also witnessed violence, genocide, and evolutionary disaster.

But if America has changed the West, the West has also permeated the very fabric of American life. Its wild and beautiful landscape is familiar around the planet, to millions who have never breathed its free air. As well as its massive impact on American culture, the movies, literature, fashion, and playthings, the West has become an idea. It has come to represent the very best of America itself: freedom, courage, and self-determination.

For everyone who loves the Old West, The Wild West Catalog is a virtual tour around the most extraordinary century in the region's history. The book recreates its drama, iconography, atmosphere, and most fascinating of all, its cavalcade of legendary characters.

THE COWBOY

Out where the handclasp's a little stronger,
Out where the smile dwells a little longer,
That's where the West begins;
Out where the sun is a little brighter,
Where the snows that fall are a trifle whiter,
Where the bonds of home are a wee bit tighter,
That's where the West begins.

From Arthur Chapman's "Out Where the West Begins"

Oh, he would twirl that lariat and he didn't do it slow
He could catch them forefeet nine out of ten for any kind
  of dough
And when the herd stampeded he was always on the spot
And he set them to milling, like the stirrings of a pot.

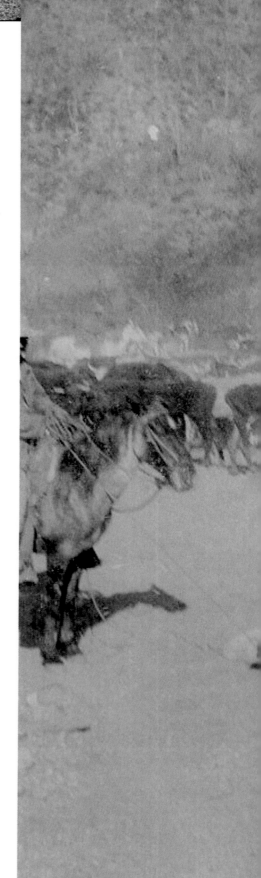

Right: Cowboys roping a steer

Of all the West's iconic characters, perhaps the cowboy is the most universally recognized and admired. But, ironically, the role that has come to symbolize the free spirit of America actually originated in Spain. The Conquistadors brought their cowboy skills to South America in the sixteenth century; the *vaqueros* herded large numbers of horses and cattle across the open lands to forage. These original "cowpunchers" were usually mounted on horseback, but also used donkeys, or *burros*. "Cowboy," the English-language equivalent of the Spanish term made its first appearance between 1715 and 1725. By this time, the cattle industry was becoming an increasingly important element of the North American economy, particularly in the South and West. "Boy" was by no means meant to demean. Tough work like this required youth and vigor, and real boys as young as twelve were employed in ranch work. As European settlers brought longhorn cattle to the New World, a culture of ranching became established, particularly in the South. Ironically, the market for beef was very limited at this time, and the animals were mainly bred for their hides and tallow.

Above: The Texas Longhorn, a breed that was well suited to the arid conditions of the Southwest.

Left: The original cowboy was the Spanish Vaquero, shown here in a sketch by Frederick Remington.

Right: Abilene, the archetypal cow town, as it was in the early 1880s.

The state of Texas (independent from 1836), soon became prominent in the American cattle trade. Anglo-Texans drove out many Mexican ranchers and confiscated their animals. This new breed of cattlemen soon developed its own cowboy-ing traditions. Typically, the Texas cowboy was single, a solitary drifter, who worked for a different outfit every season. By contrast, the Californian "cowboy tradition" was for men to live on permanent ranches. More verdant grazing meant that there was less open range, and Californian meat tended to stay in the region, which meant far fewer cattle drives. The Californian ranching system dated back many years. There were already nineteen *rancheros* by 1790, and this number was greatly increased by 1836. Spanish mission farmlands were seized by the Mexican government, and redistributed, often in huge tracts, to favored ranchers as grazing land.

California's ranch-based cowboys (also known as "buckaroos") had a much more settled, domestic existence than their Texan counterparts, and were considered more skilled in animal husbandry. Because their lifestyles were more predictable, and less dangerous, many of these men married, settled on their home ranches, and raised families

Above: An obviously posed picture of a roped steer in Graham County, Arizona in the 1890s.
Left: An Australian Stockman tends his herd in the outback.

Right: A Paiute Indian shows his skill in roping; many Native Americans became successful cowboys.

there.

A third class of cowhand, the Florida cowhunter, or "cracker cowboy" had a completely different modus operandi. Spanish settlers had introduced cattle to the state in the sixteenth century, and the cowhunters themselves were usually of Spanish or Indian origin. These men used dogs and bullwhips, rather than Western lassos, to control the smaller breeds of cattle native to this region. Historically,

meat produced in Florida was used to supply the Spanish missions in the north of the state, and the island of Cuba, but became of critical importance to the Confederacy during the Civil War. It was so important that in March of 1864, the 800-strong "Cow Cavalry" (the 1st Battalion Florida Special Cavalry) was formed to protect the cattle from Union raiders.

The cowboy tradition also developed outside the United States. The Canadian cattle industry was focused on Alberta and Saskatchewan, and many of its cowboys were American. Elsewhere, Hawaii had its *paniolos*; Argentina its *gauchos*; Peru its *chalans*; Chile its *huasos*; Mexico its vaqueros and charros; and Australia its stockmen and drovers. Each of these regions had wide-open spaces for grazing cattle, sheep, or horses, and generated their own herding techniques and traditions.

Wherever cowboys worked, the life was almost always hard, potentially dangerous, and lonely. The pay was meagre, and at the time the profession carried a lowly social status. Their melancholy permeated the rich cowhand culture of songs and poems.

The defeat of the Southern states in the Civil War had a great effect on the cattle industry, leading to a kind of cowboy diaspora. When Texans went off to fight in the war, their cattle were left to roam free, and huge herds had built up. There was now no market for the five million cattle stranded in the economically crippled South, while the industrial North was desperate for meat. To drive the cattle north was extremely difficult, time-consumin, and dangerous, and this meant that cowboy skills were in high demand. The Civil War also had had a strong impact on the racial mix of the men following the profession. Many freed slaves were attracted to the freedom of riding the range, and as many as 5,000, one-quarter of the men riding the line in Texas were African-Americans. Mexicans also became cowboys, as did men from several Native American tribes including the Creeks, Seminoles, and Timucuas.

Originally, the Texan herds were driven across Missouri on their way to the north and east, but the cattlemen ran into increasing hostility from the local farmers, who objected to the damage caused by the drives. Many also believed that the cows carried a virulent tick that was deadly to their livestock.

In effect, this standoff meant that thousands of cattle were marooned in Texas, where they were worth only $4 a head, and prevented from moving to the more industrialized parts of the nation, where they could be sold for in excess of $40 a head. This economic opportunity was not lost on entrepreneurial cattlemen like Joseph G. McCoy, who

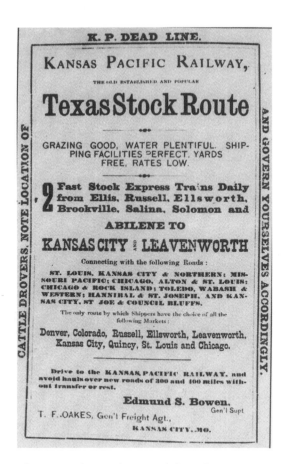

Above: A guide to cattle trails produced by the Kansas Pacific Railway.

Below: The main street at Ellsworth in 1872.

persuaded the Kansas Pacific Railroad to build a siding at Abilene, Kansas. He then constructed a huge complex of stockyards, where cattle could be held before being directly loaded onto the eastbound railroad. He then encouraged the Texan ranchers to bring their stock to Abilene.

In 1867, he was responsible for shipping 35,000 head of cattle, but this was to increase exponentially to 600,000 head in 1871. One of the main routes used by the herders to get to McCoy's Abilene stockyards was the Chisholm Cattle Trail. This dirt track route was named for Jesse Chisholm. Chisholm had built several trading posts, before the outbreak of the Civil War, alongside what was to become the Oklahoma section of the Trial. Sadly, Jesse Chisholm died in 1868, and never drove cattle along the route that bore his name. The first cattleman to use the Trail, to drive Texan cattle from San Antonio to the railhead at Abilene, was O. W. Wheeler. In 1867, Wheeler succeeded in herding 2,400 steers along the route to Abilene. Ultimately, Chisholm's dirt track was to be trodden by upwards of five million cattle, and a million mustangs. It became a hugely important financial artery, and aided in the recovery of the South from the devastating effects of the Civil War.

In its original form, the Trail began in Texas, at San Antonio, and ended at the Kansas town of Abilene. But it gradually extended further into Kansas, first to Newton, then to Wichita, and finally to Caldwell (by 1883). The long drive from Texas to Kansas took between two and three months,

Real Texas Cowboys

Right: George Dickerson Callaway Sr. drove cattle on the Chisholm Trail in the 1880's.

William Theodore Callaway and his brother George Dickerson Callaway were drivers along the Chisholm Trail, beginning in 1867. They drove cattle for many years until they both got married and settled down. George married an Oklahoma girl and was listed in the 1900 census as residing in Woodward County, Oklahoma Territory.

William became a trail boss in 1873 and continued until he made his last trip in 1882.

He married Mary E. Miller in 1871, finally settling in Wilson County, Texas.

William Callaway was Democratic Party Chairman for Wilson County for 15 years.

Right: William Theodore Callaway, brother of George, who made his last drive in 1882.

Right: Classic round-up scene taken at the Sherman Ranch in Kansas.

Left: Map showing the synergy between the railroads and cattle trails.

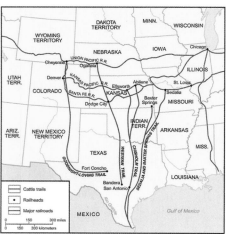

Right: The Southwestern Hotel in Caldwell, Kansas in the early 1880s. Caldwell was a major cowtown.

Left: A dusty cattle herd being driven along the trail. They moved at around 10 to 12 miles per day.

and was enough to challenge even the most experienced and accomplished Texas cattlemen. The cattle moved along at around ten to twelve miles a day, which allowed them to graze as they went. The terrain itself was extremely difficult. The herdsmen had to drive the cattle across two major rivers (the Arkansas and the Red), together with various creeks, canyons, mountains, and badlands along the route. But ruthless cattle rustlers and predatory Native Americans (Oklahoma was still Indian Territory at this time) probably caused the cowboys more sleepless nights along the drive. There was also an ever-present danger of stampede from the capricious Texan Longhorn.

The mastering of these diverse problems greatly enhanced the reputation of the Texas cowboy, and he achieved an almost folkloric status. Specialist trailing contractors managed most of these drives, and they recruited bands of cowboys to ride the line. Over the years, these trail bosses perfected an economic system of cattle driving that meant they could get the animals to market for around sixty to seventy-five cents a head. This was far cheaper than sending the cattle by rail. These highly skilled professional drovers included rugged individuals like John T. Lyle, George W. Slaughter, and the Pryor brothers.

The Great Western Cattle Trail ran roughly parallel, to the Chisholm Trail, to the West. It ran from Bandera, Texas to Dodge City, Kansas. Doan's Crossing was the last supply post on the Trail before the lands of the Indian Nation. C. E. Doan was the proprietor of the trading post there, and kept a tally of the beasts moving through. The peak of the traffic occurred in 1881, when 301,000 head of cattle passed through. The largest individual herd to go through consisted of 10,000 animals. But the Trail became increasingly dangerous as the Cheyenne and Arapaho tribes were confined to reservations. Now that the wild antelope and buffalo were nearly extinct, being restricted to these "meatless" lands effectively meant a lingering starvation for the natives. They tried to survive by demanding a "trail bounty" of beef from each passing herd. If the trail bosses refused to pay, the Indians retaliated by making attacking the drive, or making their cattle stampede.

Perhaps the most famous trail route of all was the Goodnight-Loving Trail. Charles Goodnight and Oliver Loving formed a partnership when they met in 1867, and instigated a cattle drive from Young County in Texas to Fort Sumner in New Mexico. Thousands of Native Americans were confined to a reservation there, and were starving for

Left: The extinction of the buffalo led Native Americans to steal cattle from the drives.

Right: Charles Goodnight, the greatest Western cowboy of them all. He lived on a diet of coffee, beef and Cuban cigars.

the want of meat. Oliver Loving went to scout a route for the cattle to follow, but was shot by a Comanche brave, and died of septicaemia.

The Goodnight-Loving Trail originally ran southwest to the Horsehead Crossing on the Pecos River to Fort Sumner, but in 1871, Goodnight extended the route to join up with the Forth Worth and Denver City Railroad at Grenada, Colorado, and many cattle were sold to gold diggers. Ultimately, the Trial went as far as Cheyenne, Wyoming. Charles Goodnight had a huge influence on the culture of the West, and is even credited with having coined the modern use of the term "cowboy." He had a close, almost paternal, relationship with his men, and forbade them to drink, swear, or play cards. This inveterate plainsman was a cattle industry pioneer, and made a huge contribution to the hugely lucrative and practice of driving cattle to market. One of his most important innovations was the invention of the iconic chuck wagon. Cattlemen like Goodnight changed the fortunes of the whole region. He died at his ranch at the age of 93, having survived for years on a diet of coffee, beef, and Cuban cigars.

The heyday of the cattle drives and the trails they used was

between 1866 and 1890. Originally, the drives were a major stimulant to the burgeoning railroad network, but as the tracks extended into previously uncharted territory, the need for long and dangerous cattle drives was gradually diminished. They were virtually redundant by the 1890s. The advent of refrigerated cars in the 1880s meant that fresh beef could be transported all the way to Europe by ship.

A combination of railroad expansion, the introduction of Joseph F. Glidden's "Devil's Rope" (barbed wire, patented by him in 1874), and irrigation windmills gradually began to tame the Western plains. It was barbed wire that finally closed down the Chisholm Trail in 1884, and vastly reduced the open routes of virtually all the Western Trails.

These inventions resulted in a shift away from the open range towards fenced-in ranching, a move which was hastened by the terrible meteorological events of 1886 and 1887. A combination of the desperate overgrazing of the prairie (by an estimate 35 to 40 million animals) and

Above: "The Devil's Rope," barbed wire, was patented by Joseph F. Glidden in 1874.

Above right: An early ranch with wooden stockading.

atrocious weather conditions led to an ecological disaster. There was an extreme drought in the spring of 1886, following by a scorching summer, where temperatures on the prairie reached over 109 degrees Fahrenheit. In January 1887, there was a tremendous winter storm, and temperatures fell lower than minus 43 degrees Fahrenheit. A devastating famine ensued, and it is estimated that over half the cattle on the prairies died. Many cowboys also perished from cold and hunger. Effectively, the days of the wide-open spaces were numbered, and many cattle operations were bankrupted. The need for private individuals to manage the land properly meant that ranching became much more widespread, and publicly owned grazing land was gradually enclosed. This change in the way the prairie was managed was also helped by the pacification of the Plains tribes. Positively, it somewhat halted the decimation of the wild buffalo. This more business-like approach meant that ranches became sound financial investments for cow-savvy entrepreneurs and their financial backers, such as Charles Goodnight and his investor John G. Adair. Huge fortunes were made, and it is estimated that by 1885, just thirty-five cattle barons owned 1.5 million cattle among them. About two-thirds of the Western lands were now being used for grazing.

Not everyone was happy about the cattle ranchers' domination of this entire region. Writing in 1955, Bernard

Above: The interior of a bunkhouse shows what extremely Spartan lives ranch-based cowboys lived, but life was easier than on the trail.

DeVoto wrote a damning description of this system. "The cattlemen came from Elsewhere into the empty West. They were always arrogant and always deluded… They kept sheepmen out of the West… [and] did their utmost to keep the nester, the farmer, the actual settler, the man who could create local and permanent wealth out of the West… the big cattlemen squeezed out the little ones wherever possible… frequently hiring gunmen to murder them."

This move to ranching also led to a changing focus for cowboys, who became more orientated towards animal husbandry than herding. Their new duties included feeding, branding, ear marking, and basic veterinary care. They were also responsible for maintaining the ranch-land, its water supply, and its boundaries.

One of the most recognisable aspects of the classic American cowboy was (and still is) his outfit and paraphernalia. His kit evolved over many years, and was driven by practicality. Many of its constituent parts were based on the original outfit of the Mexican vaqueros.

Traditionally, the cowboy wore a wide-brimmed hat to protect his face from the sun and snagging branches. It was also high-crowned to keep his head cool. A "stampede string" under the chin kept the hat in place in windy weather or during rough riding. The most famous maker of this kind of headgear was John Batterson Stetson, a professional hatter who popularised a felted version, the "Boss of the Plains," with Western cowboys. The hat was so successful, that Stetson built a large national corporation on the its popularity. It was worn, and popularized, by a number of Western luminaries, including Buffalo Bill, Annie Oakley, Calamity Jane, and Will Rogers.

Around his neck, the correctly attired cowboy wore a bandanna. This was a large silk or cotton cloth (usually 36 to 44 inches square) that could be used to mop the face, or keep the dust out of his mouth. This neckerchief was also known as a "wild rag" or mascada, and was often elaborately

Stetson

Mexican sombrero

Stetson

Bandana

cowboy spurs

Buerman spur

Soft felt hat

Spurs

Boots from the 1890s

One-piece cowboy boots
from the 1870s

Fringed hide gloves

Left: An early photograph of Will Rogers, complete with lariat.

Studded leather wrist cuffs

Sheepskin-lined coat

knotted. On his feet, the cowboy wore high-topped boots to protect his lower leg from chafing, during long hours in the saddle. The narrow toes helped the cowboy to get his feet into the stirrups, while the high heels kept them there. Many of these boots were also equipped with spurs, to give the rider a stronger leg action. Western spurs are made from metal, and often have a small, serrated wheel attached to them. This was known as the rowel, *la rodaja* or *la estrella* in Spanish.

Most cowboys wore sturdy jeans to prevent tangling with brush or equipment, and were among the first groups of Americans to popularize this practical form of clothing. Levi Strauss opened his eponymous company in San Francisco in 1853, and gained a patent for his famous reinforcing rivet in 1873. The inside leg seams of real cowboy jeans were rolled so that they wouldn't rub his legs on horseback. Further protection was offered by leather chaps, or chinks (known in Spanish as *las chaparreras* or *chaparejos*), which were worn over the jeans. These came in many varieties, tailored to the local conditions. Angora chaps, for example, which were covered in long goat hair, were worn for warmth in Wyoming and Montana. Other varieties included batwing chaps, shotgun chaps, woolly chaps, short chaps, and *armistas* chaps. On his hands, the cowboy wore thick hide gloves, to protect his hands from the weather, rope, barbed wire, tools, brush, and vegetation. He might also have a pair of leather wrist cuffs to protect his shirtsleeves. Like the iconic leather jacket worn by many cowboys, these gloves might well be dandified by the addition of long leather fringes. For bad weather, the cowboy might also have a slicker or "pommel

Buffalo and leather chaps

slicker." This was a long, waterproof coat, designed to protect both the saddle and rider.

The cowboy also had a modest supply of professional equipment, including a quart (a horsewhip made from braided leather), a lariat (known as a *riata* when made from hide, or a *sogo* when made from plant fiber), a leather rope strap, and a bedroll of rolled up blankets. This was also called a dreaming sack.

Although cowboys might have aspired to carry expensive pistols, their weapons were more likely to be ex-Civil War guns, like the Spencer Repeating Rifle. For the slightly better off, the ultimate cowboy weapon was Winchester's 1866 Carbine. This somewhat more sophisticated weapon used rim fire cartridges, and its compact (twenty-inch) barrel made it easy for a cowboy to stow the gun in his saddle scabbard. With no bolt action, or any other encumbrance, it was swift to draw, and fire straight from the saddle; and just as easy to replace. Larger barrelled guns, such as the Henry Rifle, were also highly regarded on the plains.

As well as warding off trouble, cowboys used their weapons to control varmints and shoot game. Heavier rifles, like the Sharps and Spencers were often used for larger prey, like buffalo.

Knives were also an intrinsic part of every cowboy's equipment, and many carried the famous Bowie knife. Jim Bowie had originated his uniquely curved blade in the very early years of the nineteenth century. The knife was designed specifically to be a combined weapon and tool, for use while camping, hunting, and fishing. Bowie himself used an early version to win his famous Sandbar Fight of 1827. Over the years, he developed many versions of his uniquely curved steel blade. These varied from between six and twelve inches long, and one-and-a-half and two inches wide.

But perhaps the most important accoutrement in any cowboy's life was his horse (*caviada* or *caballa* in Spanish), and its tack. Stock horses were bred to make them as effective as possible, and their equipment was developed to suit their work. Trail drive horses were bred to be small and

Quart

Lariat

Levi jeans

Henry rifle

Bowie knife and sheath

light and to have good "cow sense," which meant knowing how to react to, and control, moving cattle. The Morgan, Chickasaw, and Virginia Quarter-Miler were all popular breeds. Some of these are now extinct. Their tack was developed for the comfort and practicality of men who often spent all day in the saddle. The traditional Western saddle

has a deep, secure seat with a high pommel and cantle, and is equipped with wide stirrups. Among other things, the high pommel was also used to store the cowboy's lariat. The comfort of the horse was also considered. The saddle was made with a wide saddletree that distributed the rider's weight over a greater area of the horse's back. A woollen

Above: (top) Sharps rifle, (below) Winchester Model 1866, "Yellow Boy" carbine.

horse blanket was also placed under the saddle to prevent chafing and rubbing. These were often woven by Native Americans, or imported from Mexico. At the business end, the Western bridle is usually equipped with a curb bit and has long split reins to give the rider as much control over the horse as possible. Most cowboys also had a set of leather saddlebags, also known as war bags, to accommodate their few personal belongings.

Of course, the other "equipment" that every cowboy needed was strength of mind and body. The unspoken cowboy code, of loyalty, honesty, common sense, and toughness, came to be highly regarded. A true cowboy spoke little, but meant what he said; he was a man who was strong, but chose to be gentle. These cowboy virtues have been embodied in many fictional characters, on the page and on screen, and remain powerfully attractive.

The men often formed life-long friendships out on the prairie, and a strong cowboy culture grew up around the camaraderie of the campfire. Songs, music, dancing, and poetry all formed a lively counterpoint to their hard and dangerous lives. Many famous cowboy songs date from the heyday of the trail drives and cow camps, and are full of nostalgia, raw sentiment, death, fighting, and humor. The song titles are deeply evocative, and many form a part of country music culture to this day. These songs include "The Texas Cowboy," "Blood on the Saddle," "The Old Cow Man,"

Above: Trail drive horses were bred to be small and light.

Left: A variety of antique Western cowboy saddles.

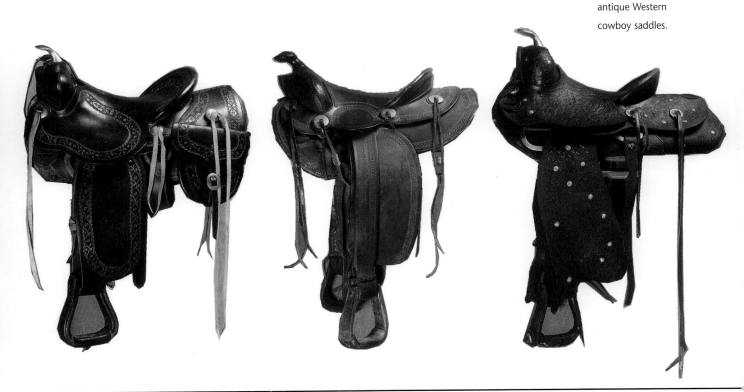

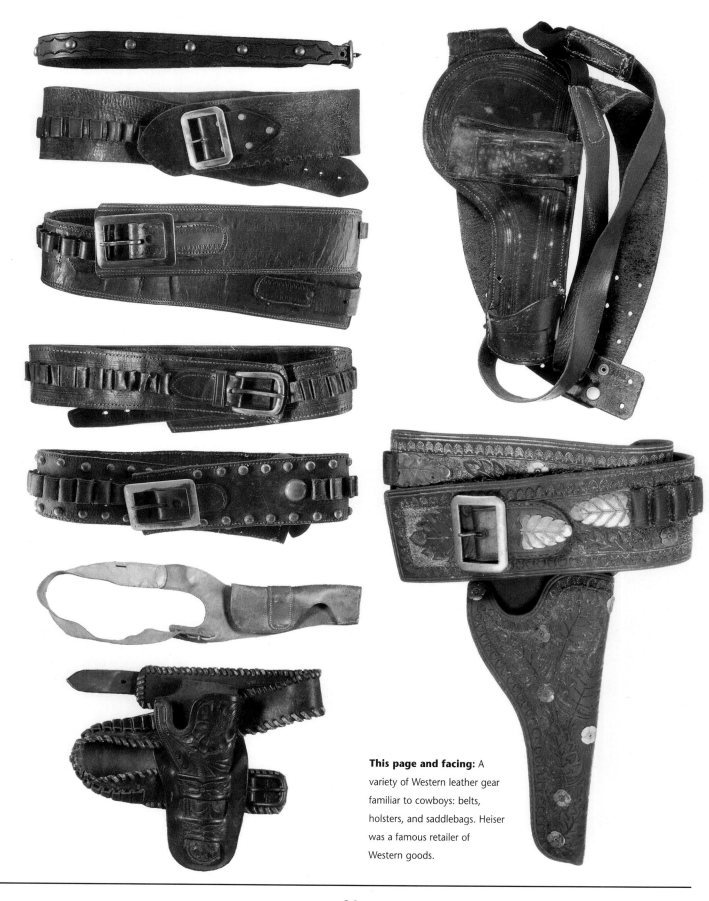

This page and facing: A variety of Western leather gear familiar to cowboys: belts, holsters, and saddlebags. Heiser was a famous retailer of Western goods.

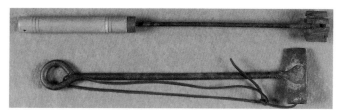

Above: Branding irons.

Above: Western saddle blanket in the Navajo style.

The cowboy lay in it, all covered with gore
Oh pity the cowboy, all bloody and dead
A bronco fell on him and mashed his head.

From "Blood on the Saddle"

Ho! Wind of the far, far prairies!
Free as the waves of the sea!
Your voice is sweet as in alien street
The cry of a friend to me!
You bring me the breath of the prairies
Known in the days that are sped,
The wild geese's cry and the blue, blue sky
And the sailing clouds o'er head.

From "The Call of The Plains"

This spirit of romanticism was actually one of the strongest

"The Streets of Laredo," "The Call of the Plains," and "The Drunken Desperado."

These assorted cowboy verses carry some hint at the different emotions carried by the songs; wistful, tragic, and funny in turns.

I'm wild and woolly and full of fleas,
I'm hard to curry below the knees,
I'm a she-wolf from Shannon Creek,
For I was dropped from a lightening streak
And it's my night to hollow – Whoo-pe!
From "The Drunken Desperado"
There was blood on the Saddle, blood all around
And a great big puddle of blood on the ground

Above: The Buffalo Bill Wild West Show arrives in Oakland, California.

surviving elements of the cowboy tradition. Exhibitions like Buffalo Bill Cody's Wild West Show (which ran between 1884 and 1906) celebrated the most entertaining and stereotypical aspects of life in the West. The entertainment included a cowboy and Indian battle, a buffalo hunt, and the Deadwood stagecoach. The show also featured real-life Western characters such as Sitting Bull, Wild Bill Hickok, and Annie Oakley. "Pawnee Bill" (Gordon W. Lillie) presented a similar Wild West show between 1888 and 1908.

This idealized view of the cowboy and his skills is still perpetuated by the modern rodeo. Although this form of entertainment now seems like a window onto the world of the traditional cowboy, it actually predates Western expansion by over a century. The first rodeos were held in the early 1700s, and celebrated the authentic cowboy chores of tie-down roping, bronc riding (broncs are unbroken horses), and team roping. "Rodeo" was a Spanish vaquero term, meaning "round-up," and did not acquire its modern meaning until 1916. The first "rodeos" were called "Cowboy Competitions," or "Cowboy Tournaments." These included the famous 101 Ranch Wild West Show, founded by Joe Miller in 1905. Brave cowgirls also participated in early rodeos, but the death of the famous Bonnie McCarroll in a 1926 bronc riding accident caused many shows to drop female events. When the Rodeo Association of America was founded in the same year, it was created as an all-male entity.

Originally, rodeos were popular with working cowboys as a means of demonstrating their skills, and supplementing their low wages. But participation in the sport has now become a profession in itself. Each year, 7,500 contestants compete for over $30 million in prize money, in over 650 American rodeos. Although only loosely based on the folkloric skills of the Western cowboy, the modern rodeo still requires extreme courage, strength, and expertise. Many events remain substantially unchanged. These include bull riding (which continues to be the most popular event), steer wrestling, calf

Above: A program for Buffalo Bill's famous Wild West Show.
Above left: A commemorative ashtray from the El Paso Hotel.

roping, and bareback bronc riding. All of these activities are as potentially dangerous as they ever were. There are now several Rodeo Associations that run the sport, and cater for various special interest groups. As a sign of how times have changed, these organizations include the International Gay Rodeo Association, The All Indian Rodeo Cowboys Association, and the Women's Professional Rodeo Association.

Above: A classic rodeo scene.

THE CHUCKWAGON

"God bless the meat and damn the skin back yer ears and dive in!"

A cowboy's invitation to dine

Cowboys eat first, talk later.
It's OK to eat with your fingers. The food is clean.
When you ride off, ride down wind from the wagon

Chuck Wagon Etiquette

Right: Cowboys cluster around the chuck wagon at the end of a hard day.

Charles Goodnight first introduced the iconic chuck wagon in 1866. Texas rancher, cattle king, and co-founder of the famous Goodnight-Loving trail, Goodnight understood the huge importance that cowhands placed on "larruping good" vittles. The first chuck wagon was constructed from wood, and drawn by oxen. The chuckbox, sited towards the rear of the wagon, had a hinged lid that dropped down to become the food preparation area. The box also contained various drawers and compartments, which held the cooking equipment (Dutch ovens, skillets, and the all-important coffee pot), together with various easily preserved staples such as corm meal, flour, dry beans, jerky, dried fruit, molasses, coffee,

Above: Canned foods became available from the 1880s.

sourdough starter, and chile peppers. Often second only in importance to the trail boss himself, the chuck wagon "cookie" not only used the materials packed in the wagon, but also foraged for locally available game and produce. Unsurprisingly, meat was a large component of the "grease hungry" cowboy diet, and although they had a ready supply of fresh beef, the trail diet was livened up with venison, wild turkey, squirrel, quail, duck, rabbit, and grouse. "Cookie" might also collect herbs (especially sage), acorns, buckwheat, nuts, greens, and wild berries along the trail.

By the 1880s, some canned goods were available to chuck wagon cooks on the northern range, including canned tomatoes, peaches, and condensed milk.

Left: A classic John Deere chuck wagon.

Right below: A selection of classic cowboy ingredients including pinto beans and chilis.

Above and left: "Cookie" preparing trail meals from the chuck wagon. The many drawers held the provisions.

Left: The closed up chuck wagon ready to roll.

Above: Cowboys posing for the camera during their meal break.

These luxuries had migrated to the southern range by the 1890s. But although "authentic" chuck wagon recipes sometimes include fresh dairy products and eggs, these were not in general use before the 1920s.

Cowboys often sought to work for the bosses with the best trail cooks, and even described their trail work as "riding the grub line." Western writers, such as Louis L'Amour, were quick to celebrate the mythical powers of chuck wagon cooks to charm the least promising ingredients into appetizing meals. Retired cowboys, who settled down to ranching,

missed not only the freedom of the trail, but chuck wagon coffee and biscuits, cooked on an open fire. Equally, less successful cooks were reviled, and heaped with unfriendly epithets, including Belly Cheater, Grub Worm, Gut Robber, and Pot Rustler. While bunkhouse cooks had access to a greater range of equipment and foodstuffs, they could not rival the esteem accorded to a good cook on the open range. Trail bosses rewarded these men with better wages than those of the regular cowboys.

Some cowboy dishes, like "Possum Roast" and "Rattlesnake Soup" may have lost their appeal, but many chuck wagon recipes still sound mighty appetizing. Here are just a few of the most well-known.

Left: Chuck wagon coffee served in enamelware.

Below: Texas Camp Bread cooked in an iron skillet.

Chuck Wagon Coffee

Take two pounds of good strong ground coffee. Put in enough water to wet it down. Boil it for two hours, then toss in a horseshoe. If the horseshoe sinks, it ain't ready.

Cowboy Sausage and Sweet Taters

2 pounds of sweet potatoes
½ cup granulated sugar
½ cup brown sugar
¼ cup water
2 tablespoons butter
1 teaspoon salt
1 pound sausages

Set a large pot of water to boil. Parboil the sweet potatoes for

15 minutes. Drain the potatoes, then peel and cut the potatoes into strips. Place them in a greased Dutch oven. Mix the sugars, butter, salt, water, and boil the mixture in a saucepan until thickened slightly. Pour the syrup over the potatoes and bake for around 40 minutes. Place the sausages on top of the potatoes and bake for an additional 30 minutes

Texas Camp Bread

This recipe dates from the 1850s.

- 10 cups flour
- 3 teaspoons salt
- 4 teaspoons black pepper
- 1 teaspoon sugar
- 1 tablespoon lard
- 4¼ cups water

Sift and mix all the ingredients together. Use lukewarm water to make fairly dry dough. Then let the dough set for 20 to 30 minutes. Roll out the dough until it is ¼ to ½ inch thick. Cut into rounds and cook on a hot, bacon greased, cast iron

skillet or Dutch oven. Prink with a fork and turn over when browned on the first side.

Lazy Corn Fritters

- 1¼ cups flour
- 2 cups corn
- 1 teaspoon baking powder
- 2 teaspoons salt
- ½ cup sugar
- ¼ teaspoon paprika
- 2 eggs
- ¼ cup milk

Mix all ingredients in a large bowl. Drop spoonfuls of the batter into a large skillet of hot oil, and fry until lightly browned.

Right: Cowboy beans

Spotted Pup Dessert

1 cup rice

Handful of raisins

¼ cup molasses

Pinch cinnamon

1 tablespoon vanilla

Put everything in a pot and bring to the boil. Stir the mixture frequently until the water is absorbed by the rice.

Chuck Wagon Beans

1 pound dry pinto beans

Handful bacon or salt pork

1 can tomatoes

1 teaspoon garlic powder

2 tablespoons chili powder

Salt to taste

Pick through the beans to remove any rocks or debris, then rinse them in cold water. Put the beans and pork in a cooking pot and cover them with cold water, two knuckles high above the beans. Cook the beans and pork until they are soft, for around 1 hour 30 minutes to 2 hours. Then add the seasonings and simmer for 30 to 40 minutes to allow the flavors to blend.

Cowboy Beans

2 cups dried red beans

2 cups dried pinto beans

1 chopped onion

3 tablespoons chopped garlic

3 green chile peppers, grilled and diced

3 tomatoes, seeded and chopped

1 tablespoon vegetable oil

7 quarts water or stock

1 smoked ham hock

1 teaspoon toasted coriander

1 bay leaf

2 whole dried red chiles

salt and pepper to taste

Above: Peach cobbler.

Above: Dutch ovens were buried in the campfire embers to cook cowboy stews.

Soak the beans in water overnight, changing the water once. Rinse and drain the beans. Sauté the onions, garlic, green chiles, and tomatoes in oil over a medium heat. Add the stock or water and the ham hock, and bring the mixture to the boil. Add the beans, coriander, bay leaf, and dried red chiles. Boil for thirty minutes, then lower the heat, cover, and simmer for three to four hours. Check that the beans are tender, then season with salt and pepper to taste. Remove the bay leaf before serving.

Peach Cobbler

On the range, a Dutch oven would be used to cook the cobbler in the campfire, at around 350 degrees.

FOR THE FILLING:
2 large cans of peaches, undrained
Cinnamon to taste

1 teaspoon vanilla

Sugar to taste

FOR THE TOPPING:

2 cups flour

½ cup sugar

1 teaspoon baking powder

½ teaspoon salt

¼ cup butter

2 to 3 cups of canned milk

Melt the butter in the bottom of the Dutch oven, pour in the peaches, and add the cinnamon and sugar. Cook briefly until the peach syrup thickens slightly.

For the topping, put the dry ingredients into a bowl and

Below: Chuck Wagon Stew.

mix. Add the butter, melted or cold. Add the milk to form a soft ball. Drop small dumpling-sized balls of dough onto the peaches. Sprinkle a little sugar and cinnamon over the mixture. Cover and bake for around 35 to 40 minutes. Lift the lid from time to time to check the progress of the cobbler.

Buffalo Steaks with Chipotle-Coffee Rub

4 buffalo steaks

3 teaspoons ground coffee

3 teaspoons ground chipotle pepper

¼ cup paprika

2 teaspoons toasted cumin seeds

3 tablespoons sugar

1 tablespoon salt

Combine the coffee, chipotle, paprika, cumin seeds, sugar, and salt. Rub the mixture into the buffalo steaks, and then grill the meat until the desired doneness.

Chuck Wagon Stew

2½ pounds cubed beef

2 tablespoons all-purpose flour

1 tablespoon paprika

1 teaspoon chili powder

2 teaspoons slat

3 tablespoons lard

2 onions, sliced

1 clove garlic, minced

28-ounce can tomatoes

3 tablespoons chili powder

1 tablespoon cinnamon

1 teaspoon ground cloves

½ teaspoon dry crushed red peppers

2 cups chopped potatoes

2 cups chopped carrots

Coat the beef in a mixture of the flour, paprika, 1 teaspoon of the chili powder, and the salt. Brown the meat in hot lard in a large Dutch oven, then add the onion and garlic and cook until soft. Add the tomatoes, the rest of the chili pepper, the cinnamon, cloves, and crushed red peppers. Cover and simmer for 2 hours. Then add the potatoes and carrots and cook the stew until the vegetables are tender, approximately 45 minutes.

Jerky

The term "jerky" comes from the method in which the meat is removed from the bones. It was "jerked" away quickly to eliminate most of the sinews. It takes around three pounds of fresh meat to make a pound of jerky.

3 pounds salt

5 tablespoons black pepper

4 tablespoons allspice

Skin one thigh of the animal, muscle-by-muscle, removing the membranes so that only moist flesh remains. Ideally, the pieces of meat should be around 12 inches long, 6 inches wide, and 2 to 3 inches thick. Rub the spice mixture into the meat, being sure to cover the meat's entire surface. Hang each piece to dry. If the sun is too hot, hang it in the shade. Never let the meat get even the slightest bit damp. Take it inside if it rains, and cover it with canvas to protect it from the dew. The meat will be at its best after a month.

Missouri-Style Barbequed Ribs

The term "3/down" refers to the weight of the ribs. In this case, each rack of 10-12 ribs weighs three pounds or less.

2 tablespoons salt

2 tablespoons chili powder

¼ cup sugar

4 tablespoons paprika

2 tablespoons ground cumin

2 racks of 3/down pork ribs

2 tablespoons fresh ground black pepper

FOR THE BASTING SAUCE:

1¾ cups white vinegar

I tablespoon salt

2 tablespoons hot pepper sauce

1 tablespoon ground black pepper

2 tablespoons sugar

Combine the salt, chili powder, sugar, paprika, cumin, and black pepper to make a barbecue rub. Rub the ribs with this mixture, then place them on a baking sheet and bake them in a 180-degree oven for three hours. The slow cooking infuses the spices, and there is no need to turn the meat. Remove the ribs from the oven. They may now be refrigerated for up to two days. Just before warming to serve, combine ingredients for the basting sauce. Use a low charcoal fire with the rack set as high as possible to grill the ribs on each side until they have a light outer crust and are heated through. For juicy ribs, coat them with the basting sauce before removing them from the grill. Slice ribs in between the bones and serve.

Indian Breakfast

15 ounces hominy

1 chopped onion

2 to 3 slices bacon, fried and crumbled

1 bell pepper, finely chopped

Dash cayenne pepper

5 beaten eggs

Above: Indian breakfast.

Sauté the hominy, chopped onion, and bacon in a large skillet. Add the cayenne and bell pepper. Cook for around 10 to 15 minutes on a medium heat. Add the beaten eggs. Stir the eggs gently, and leave the mixture on the heat until they are barely cooked. Serve immediately.

NATIVE AMERICANS IN THE WEST

I have no more land
I am driven away from home
Driven up the red waters
Let us all go
Let us all go die together

That's where the West begins.

Creek Woman

When the white man discovered this country Indians were running it. No taxes, no debt, women did all the work. White man thought he could improve on a system like this.

Cherokee saying

Right: Comanche chief Quanah Parker with his wife Tonasa in 1892, standing on the front porch of their five-bedroom house.

Above: White settlers began to arrive in the sixteenth century and soon influenced the native tribes.

Native Americans first came to America around 40,000 years ago over the frozen Bering Strait, Beringia, which formed a land bridge between Siberia and Alaska. These people came from Asia, and were of Mongolian stock. The abundant livestock of their new homeland sustained these new Americans, and attracted further immigrants. These people arrived in the East in waves, and pushed the earlier incomers further and further West and South until the entire continent was thinly populated. When the first white settlers arrived, there were around ten million Native Americans in America. They had hugely diverse cultures and lifestyles, and a complicated oral and pictorial culture. Some were hunter-gatherers. Others were farmers. Many had long traditions of producing exquisite artifacts from natural materials. It was Christopher Columbus who coined the term "Indian" for these native peoples, under the misapprehension that he had reached the Indies. It was actually San Salvador on which he landed in 1492. The new white settlers had a devastating

effect on the indigenous population. The European diseases they carried (typhus, smallpox, influenza, measles, and diphtheria) infected and killed as many as ninety-five per cent. Perhaps the one positive consequence of the incoming Conquistadors was the re-introduction of horses to America. This had a huge impact on life on the Great Plains, enabling the Native Americans to kill buffalo and other game far more effectively, and led to the invention of the travois to move their camps and possessions more quickly and easily. Negatively, horses were also used in inter-tribal warfare.

The completely antagonistic beliefs held by the new white settlers and the Native Americans soon became a source of conflict. The indigenous people were nomadic, and believed that the man belonged to the earth, not the earth to man. By complete contrast, the Europeans were bound by the

Above: Saux chief Black Hawk. Black Hawk did not believe in the ownership of land and fought to maintain tribal traditions.

conventions of property ownership, and had a settled, cooperative style of living, and organized religion. This gulf between beliefs was well put by the famous Saux chief, Black Hawk, speaking in 1831; "My reason tells me that land cannot be sold, nothing can be sold but such things as can be carried away." As more and more white settlers arrived, the process of Westward dislocation began all over again, as European settlers arrived in the East, and started to push the Native Americans further and further West. Native American culture was highly sophisticated in a different way, with its own system of geometry and a lively story-telling culture.

But the Indians were always going to be at a huge disadvantage in any conflict. They were completely out-gunned by the Europeans' superior weapons. Fundamentally,

although different problems sparked conflict, the Indian Wars were battles for land. The U. S. government believed that the buffalo-hunting Plains Indian tribes were preventing white settlement across Kansas, Nebraska, the Dakotas, Montana, Wyoming, and Colorado. President Andrew Jackson set out the agenda of the U.S. Government in the Indian Removal Act of 1830, and many Americans held the same view as General William Sherman, who asserted, "All Indians who are not on reservations are hostile and will remain so until killed off."

Native Americans saw things completely differently. The famous Sioux chief and negotiator, Spotted Tail, countered, "This war did not spring up on our land, this war was brought by the children of the Great Father." The first of these land wars was the Arikara War of 1823. The Arikaras, who were semi-nomadic farmers living in South Dakota, were attacked by the Sioux and the U. S. Army, and driven into the North of the state. The Indian Wars rumbled on for decades, and encompassed hundreds attacks, fights, and skirmishes between the Native Americans, settlers, and the U.S. Army. The most devastating period of hostilities took place between 1866 and 1890. Geographically, this warfare spread over most of the western states: Arizona, California, Colorado, Montana, North Dakota, Oklahoma, South Dakota, Texas, Utah, Washington, and Wyoming.

There were many famous battles and countless attacks, but the Indians scored very few serious hits against their white opponents. One of their few victories was the rout of Custer's Last Stand. Far more common were massacres of the Native American tribes, like that perpetrated at Wounded Knee in South Dakota, and ill treatment, such as the infamous Trail of Tears. The latter refers to the forced removal of the Cherokee Nation from Georgia west to Oklahoma, under the terms of 1825's New Echota Treaty. A string of forts was built along the route to corral the Indians, and protect the troops who forced the 1,000-mile march west. The sophisticated Cherokees, who had been so tolerant of the white settlers arriving to share their homeland, were herded like animals and died in thousands, particularly during the savagely cold winter of 1838 to 1839. Among the victims was Quatie, the wife of tribal chief John Ross.

Estimates of casualties in the Indian Wars vary tremendously, but a reasonable approximation would probably be around 45,000 Indians, and 19,000 whites. These casualties included many women and children on both sides, many of whom perished in race hate massacres. Both

sides were extremely violent and destructive. Despite this, remnants of the native inhabitants survived, but they account for only around two percent of the modern population of the U.S. The descendants of over five hundred different tribes endure, but most have lost their distinctive languages and culture.

Even a brief analysis of a few of the most prominent tribal groupings gives an insight into the great variety of traditions and lifestyle.

APACHE

Apache is the Zuni word for "enemy," but the Apache called themselves the Inde or Dine, "the people" in their Athapascan language. The Apache were the major tribe of the American Southwest, made up from nine distinct sub-tribes, and they populated Arizona, New Mexico, Oklahoma, and Texas. Related to the Navahos, and enjoying a similar way of life, their tribal deity was known as Yusan or Ussen. Despite a fairly unsettled lifestyle, the tribe often lived in wooden huts or adobe structures. They had a reputation for being fierce warriors. They had enthusiastically adopted horses from the Spanish invaders, and were experts in horsemanship, using the animals for both hunting and raiding other tribes. Geronimo was one of the most famous Apache chiefs. His capture in 1886 was hugely symbolic, and signaled the end of the Apache warrior culture. In fact, they were the last tribe to surrender to the United States government.

Opposite: Traditional Native American winter camp.

Above: Quanah Parker's mother was a captured white girl, Cynthia Ann Parker.

Below: Apache scouts armed with rifles in Arizona, 1871.

COMANCHE

The word "Comanche" comes from the Spanish phrase camino ancho, meaning "wide trail." Their mother tongue is derived from Aztec, and is related to the languages of the Shoshone, Ute, and Paiute. Originally from the Rocky Mountains, they moved onto the Plains to hunt buffalo, and became a nomadic tribe. The tribe emerged as a distinct group before 1700, when they broke away from the Shoshone tribe. The Comanche existed in dozens of autonomous groups, and expanded by capturing women and children from rival groups and assimilating them. The horse was pivotal to their lifestyle, and the Comanche introduced the animal to other people of the Plains. They had originally used dogs to pull their travois, but now used horses. The Comanche people had a traditional division of labor; the men hunted and fought, while the women brought up their children, cooked the food, and made clothes from buckskin, deerskin, buffalo hide, bearskin, and wolf skin. The tribe preferred not to eat fish or fowl, preferring game meat flavored with berries, nuts, honey, and tallow. The Comanche were a very hospitable tribe, who worshiped the Great Spirit. The tribe was run by a council of ministers, which included a "peace chief" and a "war chief." Medicine men were also influential. Their duties included naming children. The Comanches were indulgent parents who cherished their progeny. Retired warriors gathered daily in the smoke lodge. Unfortunately, like many other Native Americans, the tribe fell victim to European diseases, such as smallpox and cholera. Their population crashed from 20,000 in the mid-1800s to a few thousand by the 1870s. By the 1860s, many Comanche were confined to reservations. Their condition had deteriorated dramatically. The buffalo was virtually extinct, and their skirmishes with the U.S. Army had been devastating.

CHEROKEE

The Cherokee were one of the largest tribes of the southeast, known as the "Tsalagi" in their own language. Cherokee came from the Creek word for "people of a different speech." They had migrated from the northwest following defeats at the hands of the Iroquois and Delaware. They became a settled agricultural people, who lived in around two hundred villages. Typically, each of these consisted of between thirty and sixty dwellings, together with a large council house where the sacred fire was kept. The tribe cultivated the "three sisters" of corn, beans, and squash. They were also hunter-gatherers, with a highly sophisticated standard of living. The Cherokee were heavily influenced by white settlers, and invented their own written language, consisting of 86 characters, in 1821. The Cherokee also traded with the British. But a devastating smallpox epidemic in 1753 killed half the tribe. They also fell out with their British allies and the Cherokee warriors massacred the garrison at Fort Loudon in eastern Tennessee in 1760. Trying to protect their valuable lands from white settlement, the tribe sold the land of other tribes. An honest Cherokee chief took Daniel Boone aside and told him "We have sold you much fine land, but I am afraid you will have trouble if you try to live there." But fighting between the tribe and white settlers continued unabated, exacerbated when gold was discovered on their lands. The Indian Removal Act of 1821 stripped the Cherokee of any legal protection, and they became the victim of every kind of theft and violence. They were finally driven to surrender their homelands in return for $5,000,000 and seven million acres of land in Oklahoma. But the treaty proved to be a fraud. The Cherokee were driven out of their lands by force, and embarked on the infamous "Trail of Tears." Many died of measles, whooping cough, and dysentery, while others perished from exposure. In the end, they were forced to abandon even the Oklahoma territory they had been awarded. The tribe was finally compensated by

Left: A Navajo war captain wearing a war hat of tanned leather, and carrying a lance and rawhide shield.

Left: A Navajo mother and child wearing silver and turquoise jewellery.

the U.S. government in 1961, with a payment of $15 million.

THE NAVAJO

The Navajo remain the largest Native American tribe, with around two hundred thousand surviving members. Navajo comes from the Spanish for "people with big lands." The tribe called themselves the "Dine" or "people." The originally came from Northwest Canada and Alaska, but traveled to the Southwest part of America. The tribe grew corn, beans, squash, and melons and wove attractive rugs and fabrics. The Navajo lived in fairly substantial houses, called hogans, made

from wooden poles, tree bark, and mud. Traditionally, the doors always opened to the East. When the white settlers arrived, the tribe stole their sheep and horses, and integrated both animals into their tribal lives. The Navajo nation now extends into Utah, Arizona, and New Mexico. It extends over 27,000 square miles, and is larger than several U.S. states.

THE SIOUX

"Sioux" is the name given to the tribe by French fur traders who had close relations with them in the late seventeenth century. It was the traders' representation of the tribe's Indian

hang for their part in the killing spree, but President Lincoln reduced this number to thirty-eight. Despite this, the resulting hanging at Mankato, Minnesota remains the largest mass execution in U.S. history. A vicious cycle of murder and revenge continued, with Red Cloud's War. Subsequent hostilities broke out in the Black Hills, including the rout and killing of Custer and his men. In 1890, the tribe's famous Ghost Dance ritual culminated in more murder and mayhem, and resulted in the death of Sitting Bull, as he tried to protect the tribe's independence. This, in turn, provoked the fight at Wounded Knee Creek, against the forces of the U.S. Seventh Cavalry.

Beaten by U.S. Government forces, the Sioux were mostly confined to reservations by the end of the nineteenth century. Confined, the tribe reverted to the farming traditions of their past, raising cattle and corn, rather than hunting the almost extinct buffalo. Most famous Sioux, including Little Crow, Crazy Horse, Red Cloud, and Sitting Bull were known for their fighting prowess, but the tribe was also noted for its dancing and fine craftwork.

Above: a famous photograph of Sitting Bull, a Sioux warrior chief known for his fighting prowess.

name, "Nadouessioux," or the "little snakes." The tribe was a large and disparate racial group, composed of three distinct ethnic strains. The Sioux migrated to the Plains in the late eighteenth century, and substantially changed their way of life from being canoe men, and gatherers of wild rice to horse-riding hunters. Largely through trading with the French, many Sioux braves also became armed with guns. The Sioux involved themselves in many pointless struggles with other tribes, but also began to attack settlers to the area. The "Minnesota outbreak" of 1862 resulted in widespread Sioux violence, and several hundred settlers were brutally murdered. A court marshal condemned 300 tribesmen to

Above: Sioux Chief Hollow Horn Bear, who as a young man fought with Sitting Bull at the Battle of Little Big Horn.

Right: An 1885 posed studio portrait of Sitting Bull and William F. Cody, alias Buffalo Bill. Sitting Bull was one of the major attractions in Cody's Wild West Show.

NATIVE AMERICAN ARTIFACTS

✵ ✵ ✵ ✵ ✵ ✵

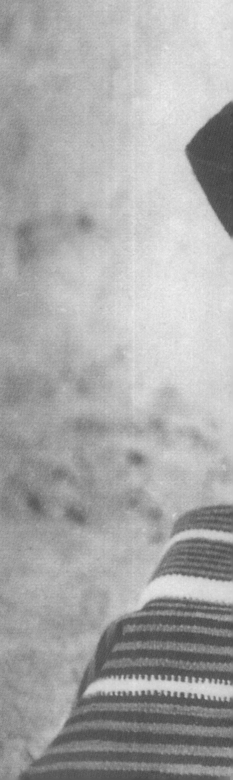

One of the most fascinating aspects of Native American life was the extraordinary range of artifacts the different tribes produced. Each group sourced their materials from their home environment, so that their work reflected the character of the region. Inevitably, the chattels of the Plains Indians reflected their close links with the buffalo, and other local game. Buffalo hide, eagle feathers and claws, mink fur, ermine fur, bone, deerskin, porcupine, otter skins, shells, stones, and gourds all feature in their work. Plateau and Basin tribes were famous for their fabulous beadwork, woven cornhusk bags, and emblematic painting. The more settled farming tribes of the Southeast also used animal-sourced materials, but were also expert weavers, basket makers, and potters. In the Southeast, fabric garments and stitching techniques (especially appliqué) were popular art forms.

Each tribe produced everything its members needed for a comfortable life, including tipi covers, clothes, weapons, travois, bedding, cradles, and cooking pots. But far beyond the ordinary necessities of life, the handwork of the indigenous peoples developed an incredible complexity of decoration, color, and subtle design cues that reflected their socially intricate way of life. Each tribe tended to have its own particular craft specialty, and unique style or ornamentation.

Right: Governor Ahfitche of San Felipe Pueblo using a pump drill to make holes in shells (1880).

The beautiful rawhide Dance Rattle belonged to Crazy Crow, a member of the Plains Indian Crow tribe. Crow braves were active buffalo hunters until the herds became extinct. The tribe fought in the Indian Wars, and subsequently became farmers in their reservation years. Dancing was an integral part of the Crows' preparation for war. The tribe had a complex social structure, with several mystical organizations, such as the Tobacco Society, open to both men and women.

Jenny LaPointe made these Lakota Sioux moccasins. They date from around 1900. Like Iron Tail, Jenny LaPointe was a member of Buffalo Bill's Wild West show. In an age of great showmen, Frontiersman Cody embroidered his experiences of hunting and warfare to inspire several revues. His shows toured the world for over twenty-five years. Over twelve hundred performers appeared in these "entertainments," including several famous Westerners, such as Wild Bill Hickok and Annie Oakley. Despite his rough-hewn image, Cody favored rights for Native Americans, and women. He died in 1917.

This magnificent war bonnet belonged to Iron Tail. Iron Tail was an Oglala Sioux, who fought alongside Sitting Bull at the Battle of the Little Big Horn. He also led the procession of Buffalo Bill's Wild West show performers on their English tour. When Cody's troupe visited the English south coast city of Hastings, the young Archie Belaney saw the show. Belaney later transformed himself into the famous "Indian" Grey Owl, and became an adopted member of the Ojibwa tribe.

Above: An oil painting by Cincinnati artist, John Hauser Jr. [1859-1918] shows Sioux Chief Iron Tail actually wearing this bonnet. A survivor of the Wounded Knee Massacre, Iron Tail's photographic image was used on the Buffalo Nickel, which was in circulation from 1913-1938.He died in 1955 aged 99.

This beaded buckskin jacket, decorated with a horse motif, was produced by Lakota Sioux craftspeople, around 1890. The Lakota Sioux were a Central Plains tribe, and the most Western of all the Sioux Indians.

This necklace of eagle claws belonged to tribesman Rough Hair. Eagles were highly respected by the Native American peoples, respected for their power, strength, and excellent vision. Some tribes kept captive eagles in cages to harvest their valuable plumage. The Sioux particularly prized eagle talons. Valuable objects like this eagle claw necklace have also been found at tribal burial sites.

THE US CAVALRY

"The only true role for cavalry is to follow the enemy as long as he retreats."

Stonewall Jackson, 1862

Right: A Union cavalryman in the Civil War.

One of the most iconic organizations active in the taming of the West and the settlement of the Frontier was the United States Cavalry. Many of the West's most famous characters served in cavalry regiments, including Buffalo Bill Cody, who served as the highly successful chief scout of the 5th Cavalry. The role of scout was absolutely vital to cavalry regiments, protecting them from ambush, and guiding them to victory.

The earliest northern-based cavalry regiment, the Philadelphia Light Horse, was formed in 1774, during the American Revolution. The regiment often served as George Washington's personal bodyguard, and went on to serve the Union in the Civil War, fighting at Bull Run and Gettysburg.

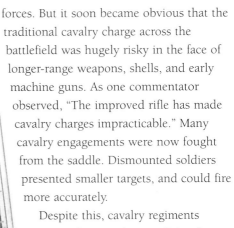

An almost exactly contemporary Southern cavalry regiment was the 1st Continental Light Dragoons. Originally known as the Virginia Light Horse, the 1st was raised in Williamsburg, Virginia, in 1776. The regiment saw Civil War action at Brandywine and Germantown. The 1st also fought the Seminole Indians in the Florida Everglades and was involved in the Mexican wars, making a famous charge on the Mexican position at Resaca de la Palma on May 9, 1846.

During the Civil War, cavalry regiments were vital to the success of both sides, although their roles changed as the conflict rolled out. At the beginning of the conflict, cavalrymen on both sides were a focus of glamour and served to boost the morale of the opposing

Above:

A member of the Philadelphia Light Horse, formed in 1774.

forces. But it soon became obvious that the traditional cavalry charge across the battlefield was hugely risky in the face of longer-range weapons, shells, and early machine guns. As one commentator observed, "The improved rifle has made cavalry charges impracticable." Many cavalry engagements were now fought from the saddle. Dismounted soldiers presented smaller targets, and could fire more accurately.

Despite this, cavalry regiments continued to use their traditional weaponry: carbines, pistols, and sabers. Southern cavalrymen also favored shotguns. Although the cavalry's short-barreled carbines were less accurate than rifles, they were easier to handle on horseback. Sharps, Burnside, Smith, and Spencer manufactured a plethora of these single-shot, weapons for both sides. Only Union cavalry regiments still carried sabers in combat situations.

Despite the trend towards dismounted engagement, there were still incidents of cavalry versus cavalry action, such as the First Battle of Bull Run, and Elon Farnsworth's ill-fated charge on the third day of Gettysburg. In the initial stages of the war, the main role of the cavalry was now reconnaissance, which was crucial to the success of both sides. It was precisely the lack of vital cavalry intelligence that was said to have led to the Confederate defeat at Gettysburg. The cavalry on both sides also mounted highly vexatious lightening raids on communication and supply lines, and harassed retreating troops.

One of the most famous Federal proponents of the use of cavalry regiments during the Civil War was Union Brigadier General Philip St. George Cooke, who published his book Cooke's Cavalry Tactics in 1862. This training manual dealt with the "Instructions, Formations, and Movements of the Cavalry of the army and volunteers of the United States."

Cavalry warfare also had notable exponents on the Confederate side. Chief among these was Lieutenant General Nathan Bedford Forrest. Forrest developed a new style of highly mobile cavalry warfare in which armed cavalry troops charged the Federal lines, and were then able to fire into the opposition at point-blank range.

Although both sides valued the speed and mobility of the

Left: Buffalo Bill served as the chief scout for the 5th Cavalry.

Above: A Burnside carbine.

Above: A second lieutenant of the 1st and 2nd Dragoons of the Mexican War period

Above: A sergeant in the 5th or 6th Michigan Cavalry

Above: Nathan Bedford Forrest

Left: Corporal Frederich Bush of the 7th Michigan Cavalry.

Right: A Federal cavalryman of the Civil War period with a brace of Colt pistols.

Above: Custer's 7th Cavalry forces ride to Little
Big Horn in 1876.

cavalry (a cavalryman could cover an average of 35 miles in an eight-hour day), it was also recognized that mounted regiments were very expensive to equip.

This was particularly relevant to Union quartermasters. It was estimated that a Federal cavalry regiment cost over $100,000 a year to maintain. At the start of the conflict, the Federal government was obliged to procure over 600,000 horses (typically four to five-year-old mares and geldings). In contrast, Confederate cavalrymen usually supplied their own mounts. This was done under the so-called "commutation system" under which they were compensated for using their own animals, saddles, and tack.

The equipment of cavalry regiments reflected a major difference between Northern and Southern society. Horses were still the main form of personal transport in the South, while streetcars, trains, and cabs were common in the industrialized North. Also, Southern cavalry units were often formed around the nucleus of mounted "slave catcher" patrols, and other local militia. As well as being more experienced riders, these men were also used to accepting quasi-military discipline. Southern horses also had a better reputation than their Northern counterparts, due to the Southern love of horse breeding and racing. Favored Southern breeds included grade horses, quarter horses, Morgans, and Arabian horses.

But logistics soon became a problem for cavalry units on both sides of the conflict, especially the Union (with its extended supply lines), as a cavalry horse required at least ten pounds of grain each day. Both sides lost a great many horses as the conflict progressed, and were often obliged to procure replacements locally. But these untrained mounts often proved difficult, or even dangerous, in combat situations.

Both Union and Confederate cavalry units were divided into mounted "troops" of a hundred men. Two "troops" made up a squadron, while a battalion consisted of three. Union regiments consisted of twelve "troops," while Confederate regiments had ten.

Union cavalrymen began the war at a substantial disadvantage, being generally less experienced horsemen than their Southern counterparts. But over the course of the conflict, they were to become one of the most formidable fighting forces that the world had ever seen. Despite the glory to come, poor leadership, and distrust of its substantially volunteer status, meant that the Union cavalry was fairly ineffective in the early stages of the conflict. Initially, it was

Above: Men of Company I, 5th Ohio Cavalry, proudly display their Sharps carbines.

used only for reconnaissance missions, to support the artillery and infantry forces, acting as the "eyes and ears of the army."

But after the Battle of Brandy Station, the Union cavalry were to assume an increasingly offensive role. Brandy Station took place on June 9, 1863, and was to be the largest cavalry engagement of the entire War, with 21,000 mounted combatants taking part.

As the war progressed, successful cavalry leaders, like Philip Sheriden, introduced a more wide-ranging use of the cavalry, including long-range raids. Sheriden led the successful Valley campaigns of 1864, and his mounted troops chased Robert E. Lee at Appomattox. Other notable cavalry campaigns included Chancellorsville, Selma, Yellow Train, and the Peninsula. Overall, the Union cavalry made a huge contribution to the North's eventual victory. As Major McClelland remarked, "During the last two years, no branch of the Army of the Potomac contributed so much to the overthrow of Lee's army as the cavalry."

At the end of the conflict, there were a total of 272 Union cavalry regiments, and 137 on the Confederate side. Over 1.5 million horses had died during the Civil War, including cavalry, draft, and artillery animals. This loss came at a huge cost to both sides, and substantially hindered the recovery of the Southern states.

After the war, many Union cavalrymen joined the newly

Left: A postcard depicting Custer's Last Stand.

Above: Troop C, 5th US Cavalry with squatters they arrested in Indian Territory before it became Oklahoma.

formed United States Cavalry. Established regiments were re-configured, and several new ones were raised. The service itself became more professional, and the role of the cavalry became more diverse. In the immediate aftermath of the Civil War, the role of many cavalry regiments was the re-establishment of law and order in the Southern states, and the enforcement of legislation passed by the U.S. Government, especially the Reconstruction Acts of 1867 and 1868, which enforced marshal law on the Southern states, and the universal franchise. In effect, the cavalry formed part of an occupying force that governed life in the south.

The cavalry was also a major enforcer of the civil law during this period, especially in the lawless Western states. Cavalry regiments were involved in many actions to bring lawbreakers and gunmen to book, including the famous 1870 shootout between members of the 7th US cavalry and Wild Bill Hickok that took place in Hays, Kansas. The sometimes-lawman and outlaw killed one cavalry officer, and wounded another.

In 1869, President Grant appointed William Tecumseh Sherman Commanding General of the United States Army, including the cavalry. Sherman's major postbellum preoccupation was the subjugation of the Indian tribes, which he saw as a barrier to progress, and to Westward expansion. The Indian Wars were begun under his direction, and the cavalry became heavily involved in these struggles. Sherman used the same scorched earth tactics against the Native American tribes as he had employed in the Civil War. Not only did he seek military victory against his enemy, but he also wanted to deprive them of their means of survival. In the case of the Plains Indians, this meant the decimation of the buffalo.

The Indian Wars raged until the Massacre of Wounded Knee in 1890, and were the primary focus of the Plains Cavalry for over two decades. In many Western movies, the cavalry is portrayed as the salvation of innocent settlers, under threat from ruthless native killers. Their battle cry, "Charge!" and the silhouettes of cavalry officers riding to the rescue was the mainstay of hundreds of western books, shows, and films for over a century. In some cases, this image was completely accurate, but the cavalry was also an instrument of United States Government policy. This included the settlement and "civilizing" of the Western territories, and the dispossession and subjugation of the native peoples.

Above: The single action Colt .45 revolver was carried by the post-Civil War US Cavalry. The gun was also known as the "Gun that won the West."

With the benefit of historical hindsight, this remit certainly does not seem as morally sound as it did at the time. Despite this, the conduct of many cavalry actions that took place during the Indian Wars demonstrated enormous courage, daring, and fortitude.

CAVALRY REGIMENTS OF THE INDIAN WARS

The 7th United States Cavalry was undoubtedly the most famous regiment to fight in the Indian Wars. Constituted in 1866, the regiment was made up of twelve companies. Like most of the post war cavalry, its troops were armed mainly with single-action Colt .45 revolvers and modified single-shot 50 caliber Model 1865 Spencer carbines. These were based on the Spencer Model 1863 of the early Civil War era, but had shorter, twenty-inch barrels. These guns were finally replaced by the Springfield Model 1873, beginning in 1874. Although sabers were still issued, these were now largely ceremonial.

Until 1871, the 7th was based at Fort Riley in Kansas. Its mission was to enforce United States law in the subjugated South. But the regiment was also involved in anti-Indian action, including the famous 1868 Battle of Washita River. Commanded by General Custer, the 7th attacked Chief Black Kettle's Cheyenne village. Even at the time, Custer's attack on a sleeping village was controversial. The General was accused of sadism, and his men of killing women and children indiscriminately.

In 1873, the 7th U.S. Cavalry moved to its base to Fort Abraham Lincoln in Dakota Territory. The regiment's initial brief was to reconnoiter and map the Black Hills mountain range, which stretches between South Dakota and Wyoming. Custer's discovery of gold in the Black Hills, during his expedition of 1874, had a profound effect on the region. Not only did this discovery precipitate the huge social upheaval of the Gold Rush, but it also exacerbated conflict with the Sioux, Lakota, and Cheyenne tribes, who were under the leadership of Sitting Bull and Crazy Horse. Modern historians accuse President Grant of deliberately provoking war with the native peoples; he was desperate for gold-fuelled growth to lift the economy out of depression.

But victory against the Sioux and Cheyenne peoples was only achieved at a huge cost to the men of the 7th cavalry. The Battle of the Little Big Horn (June 25 to June 26 1876), also known as Custer's Last Stand, saw fifty-two per cent of the regiment fall. The final half hour of the engagement resulted in the deaths of 210 cavalrymen (258 perished all together). These included Custer himself, two of his brothers (Captain Thomas Custer, and their youngest brother, civilian scout and forage master, Boston Custer), and the Custers' nephew, Autie Reed. This rout occurred because of a highly ill-advised decision on the General's part to mount an attack on an Indian village in the Montana Territory. Every man and horse of the 7th that fought at Little Big Horn perished at the scene. The single exception was Captain Keogh's famous mount, Comanche.

Custer's Last Stand was the most devastating defeat ever suffered by the United States Cavalry, but the General's reputation remained strangely unstained, largely due to the

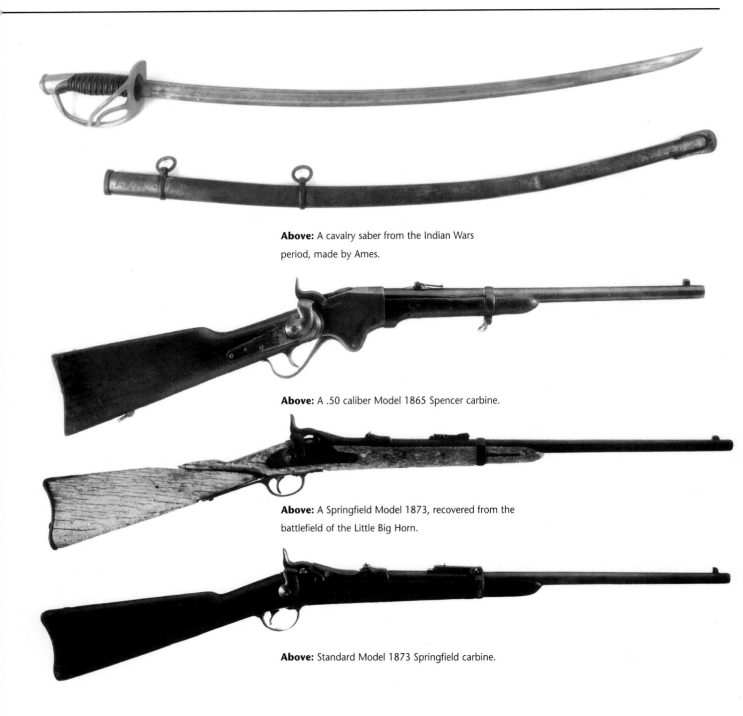

Above: A cavalry saber from the Indian Wars period, made by Ames.

Above: A .50 caliber Model 1865 Spencer carbine.

Above: A Springfield Model 1873, recovered from the battlefield of the Little Big Horn.

Above: Standard Model 1873 Springfield carbine.

efforts of his widow Elizabeth Bacon Custer and Buffalo Bill Cody. Although many commentators now place this cataclysmic defeat at Custer's feet, others point out that, by the time it took place, many cavalry recruits were malnourished and ill-trained immigrants from Ireland, England, and Prussia.

This chapter in the Indian Wars was brought to a somewhat ignominious close. Crazy Horse was promised a reservation for his weary and starving people, but this never

materialized. Ultimately, a soldier bayoneted Crazy Horse to death, as he tried to evade imprisonment.

Several other United States Cavalry regiments also fought extensively in the Indian Wars.

The 4th United States Cavalry was formed in 1855, and deployed to Texas after the war. Its main duties there were to protect settlers and the U.S. mail from Indian attack. In 1871, the regiment was called to more active duties, protecting the Texas frontier from Comanche and Kiowa attack. In March

Left: A saddle-mounted carbine boot for the 1873 Springfield.

Right: Custer with Indian scouts. His favorite Remington rifle is leaving against the guy.

Above: A cavalryman pictured in front of a native village.

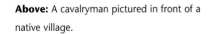

Left: Small cavalry issue folding spirit stove.

Left: The remains of Custer's valiant stand at Little Big Horn.

Right: Apache warriors, including Chief Geronimo after his surrender to US Army General Nelson A. Miles in September 1886.

Right below: The 6th US Cavalry training horses at Fort Bayard.

Right: The 6th US Cavalry practicing saber exercise at Fort Bayard.

1873, a large part of the regiment was transferred to Fort Clark, from where they made forays into Mexico to prevent highly destructive Apache raids into Texas. In 1880, the 4th was transferred to Arizona Territory, still pursuing their nemesis, the Apache. Six years later, in 1886, the 4th was instrumental in the capture of Geronimo. In 1890, the troops of the 4th were redeployed to Washington State, and took no further part in the Indian Wars. Over the period of their involvement, the regiment had had many successes against a number of Indian tribes, including the Comanches, Kiowas, Quahadi Comanches, Kotsoteka Comanches, Cheyennes, and Apaches.

The 5th United States Cavalry was raised in Louisville, Kentucky, in 1855, and was originally designated the 2nd United States Cavalry Regiment. In 1861, this regiment split between men loyal to the Confederacy and those who supported the Union. The Union cavalrymen were re-designated as the 5th, and these men were instrumental in saving their artillery at the Battle of Gaines' Mill in 1862. In the postbellum Plains Indian Wars, the regiment's main duty was to recapture escaped Sioux and Cheyenne and repatriate them to their reservations. They were also instrumental in the defeat of the Miniconjou Sioux at the Battle of Slim Buttes, which took place in Dakota Territory in 1876. Colonel Wesley Merritt led the troops in this engagement. This victory was of huge psychological importance, as it was the first significant defeat of the tribes since the annihilation of Custer's 7th.

The 6th United States Cavalry, the "Fighting Sixth" also took a major part in the Indian Wars. It was raised in 1861, and became part of the Union Army of the Potomac during the Civil War. Between 1865 and 1871, the regiment was deployed in the "Reconstruction" of Texas. The regiment also fought in the Indian Wars, and clashed with Geronimo and his Apache braves on more than one occasion.

The 8th Cavalry Regiment was formed in 1866, and organized at Camp Reynolds, Angel, California. Unsurprisingly, many of its recruits were "forty-niners," and were reputed to be pretty wild characters. The regiment's first duties were to protect the settlers and travelers of Nevada, Colorado, Arizona, and New Mexico from opportunistic attacks from Apache and Navajo tribesmen. They often provided armed escorts. The 8th also fought in the Apache Wars of southern New Mexico, and engaged with warriors from the Navajo, Comanche, and Kiowa tribes. As more settlers moved into the Northwestern states, the 8th also undertook the longest-ever cavalry march in May, 1885: 2,600 miles to their two new regimental headquarters at Ford Meade, South Dakota, and Fort Keogh, Montana.

BUFFALO SOLDIERS

African-American soldiers formed a significant part of the U.S. Cavalry in the postbellum period, and became widely known as the "buffalo soldiers." Colored regiments were constituted by the July 1866 Act of Congress, which set out how segregated regiments would "increase and fix the Current Peace Establishment of the United States."

The term was coined by the Cheyenne tribe in 1867, and

Above: A private of one of six regiments of US Colored Cavalry that were raised for the North during the Civil War. He is wearing a sky blue greatcoat, like the one on page 76.

probably referred to a combination of their admiration of the fighting ability of the black soldiers, which matched the courage and stamina shown by the buffalo, and a reference to the men's curly black hair. There were four buffalo regiments; two cavalry (the 9th and the 10th), and two infantry (the

Above: A group of buffalo soldiers pose for a photograph.

Above: A buffalo soldier re enactment.

Above: An African American buffalo soldier with bugle circa 1870s.

24th and the 25th). These soldiers became the first African American soldiers to be recruited to the army in peacetime. The men were mostly freed salves, and Civil War veterans. Over 180,000 black men had fought for the Union, and 33,000 had given their lives to the cause. These African-American soldiers were highly motivated, by a desire for respect and for recognition of their abilities. They won great admiration for their courage, and eighteen black combatants went on to receive the Congressional Medal of Honor. They wore the "buffalo soldiers" tag with pride.

Ironically, strict segregation meant that black soldiers constructed several forts and facilities that they were forbidden to use. Ultimately, the buffalo soldiers formed twenty per cent of the postbellum cavalry, and fought 177 engagements in the Indian Wars. Thirteen enlisted men and six officers from the buffalo regiments won the Medal of Honor during this period.

During the decades of the Indian Wars, the Buffalo soldiers' uniform consisted of a flannel shirt worn under a dark blue blouse, light blue trousers tucked into over-the-knee boots, together with a kepi cap decorated with the crossed saber badge and their regimental motto. The motto of the 9th was "Ready and Forward," while that of the 10th was "We Can, We Will." When mounted, the men wore a slouch campaign hat. This was black to begin with but grayish-brown after 1874. Although the Buffalo soldiers were not issued with regulation neckerchiefs, these were vital to protect them from the dust of the Plains, so most wore their

Above: Native American with Winchester Trapper carbine. Indians traded furs for repeating rifles of this kind, and effectively outgunned the Cavalry who were armed with single shot Springfield carbines.

were on duty for seven days a week, with only the Fourth of July and Christmas as holidays. Their living conditions were also grim. During the early post-Civil War years, most "forts" were actually little better than dilapidated villages. The men's living quarters were often poorly ventilated and full of vermin. This led to outbreaks of dysentery, bronchitis, and diarrhea. Despite this, morale, and standards of military discipline remained high in the black regiments. When not on duty, the men were drilled, paraded, and inspected, and were noted for the great pride they took in their uniforms.

On the positive side, Buffalo soldiers were often able to avail themselves of a rudimentary education, and although they suffered difficult living conditions, these were broadly similar to those endured by their white counterparts.

The 9th U.S. Cavalry regiment was formed in July 1866 at the instigation of General Philip Sheriden, as a segregated African-American unit. It was raised in Louisville, Kentucky, and consisted largely of men who had fought on the Union side during the Civil War. They were paid a salary of $13 per month, with their living expenses covered. The regiment was placed under the command of Colonel Edward Hatch. Its initial duty was to maintain law and order in Texas, but answering a call for help from Frank Hall, the acting governor of Colorado, fifty handpicked men from the 9th won a famous battle at Beecher Island (situated on the Arikaree River, in Yuma County, Colorado). The battle took place over three days in September 1868, and was an astonishing achievement. The small cavalry contingent overpowered a combined force of over six hundred warriors from the Arapaho, Cheyenne, Brule, and Oglala Sioux tribes, suffering only six fatalities.

Between 1875 and 1881, the regiment went on to become increasingly involved in the Apache Wars. Their distinguished service included the heroic Battle of Tularosa, where twenty-five cavalrymen fought off over a hundred Apache warriors until reinforcements arrived.

The 10th cavalry regiment was also a segregated African-American unit, and was also founded in 1866. Its headquarters were at Fort Leavenworth, Kansas. The regiment drew its recruits from Missouri, Arkansas, and the Platte (a large area which consisted of Iowa, Nebraska, Dakota Territory, Utah Territory, and part of Idaho). These men were of a notoriously high standard, and took over a year to gather together. The regiment was led by white officers, and headed by Civil War hero Benjamin Henry Grierson, who had a great belief in the black soldiers he had

own chosen neckerchief, which was usually yellow, red, or white. Like their white counterparts, the Buffalo soldiers were armed with Springfield carbine rifles, Colt Single-Action Army Revolvers (Model 1873) in .45 caliber, and traditional cavalry sabers.

The army's Buffalo cavalry and infantry regiments numbered around 5,000 men, and formed at least ten per cent of the soldiers who guarded the Western frontier, that ran between Montana to Arizona. This duty lasted for quarter of a century, between the end of the Civil War and the end of the Indian Wars in 1891. By this time, the West was considered to have been "won."

Day-to-day life for Buffalo soldiers was tough. Their rations were limited to beef, bacon, potatoes, beans, and a few fresh vegetables, with fruit or jam as an irregular treat. The men

recruited. For the next eight years, Grierson's men were based at several different forts in Kansas and Oklahoma. Their duties included protecting the men building the Kansas and Pacific railroad, which eventually ran between Kansas City and Denver. The railroad had a huge impact on the life of the West, and facilitated settlement of the Great Plains. The 10th also built a considerable part of the region's telegraphic network, and built much of Fort Sill. But they were also involved in direct combat with various Indian tribes, including the Cheyenne, Comanche, and Arapaho. They supported Sherman's winter campaigns of 1867 and 1868, and assisted Custer to gain victory at Fort Cobb.

In 1875, the regiment was moved to Fort Concho in Texas. This marked a return to duties protecting the state's infrastructure, scouting unmapped territory, opening up new roads, and extending the telegraphic network. In other words, their brief was to help civilize and tame this new territory, making it suitable for settlement. They were also the

Left: Confederate cavalry officer's coat, 1861.

Right: Butternut trousers of the kind used by Confederate cavalrymen.

main lawgivers in the area, controlling outlaws, Indians, and Mexican revolutionaries.

Between 1879 and 1880, the 10th was heavily involved in the Apache Wars, especially against the warriors of Apache chief, Victorio, a violent protégé of Geronimo, credited with the Alma Massacre of several settlers in April 1880. The regiment's most notable engagements took place at Tinaja de las Palmas and Rattlesnake Springs. They forced Victorio to retreat into Mexico, where he was finally killed by Mexican troops on October 14, 1880.

Despite the harsh discipline and conditions to which the men of the 10th cavalry were subjected, the regiment had the lowest desertion rates in the United States Army. The general desertion rate from the army was extremely high at this time, (in 1868, it was around twenty-five per cent), but it was four times higher in white regiments than among the Buffalo soldiers. Alcoholism was also much less common in black regiments.

CAVALRY UNIFORMS

"The ideal uniform should be of such character as to cause the officer and soldier who wears it to be proud of it for itself, aside from that which it typifies."

Captain Oscar F. Long, 1895

At the outbreak of the Civil War, cavalrymen on both sides were equipped with many disparate outfits. These often belonged to the militia groups in which they had served, or from various military academies.

But Union quartermasters soon began to standardize Federal uniforms. The uniform sported by the 3rd Regiment of the New Jersey Volunteer Cavalry was fairly typical of mounted Federal regiments. It consisted of sky blue cloth pantaloons adorned with yellow side stripes, a dark blue jacket with a standing collar, decorated with yellow cords (epaulettes, shoulder-knots, and chevrons) sewn onto orange grounds, and complete with three burnished buttons, together with a dark blue cap braided in yellow (or a dark colored forage cap). The final addition was a sky blue talma (or cloak), lined in yellow, and closed with fabric tabs. Many regiments were also issued with a sack coat of dark blue flannels for fatigue purposes. This was loose cut, and fastened with four buttons. The officers' coats were in dark blue, and the enlisted men wore sky-blue.

Before 1862, the Confederate cavalry uniform took many forms. Many of these were derived from homemade and often

Left: US Cavalry enlisted man's uniform of the 1870s.

Right: Cavalry hat of the 1870s with acorn tassels.

Right: US cavalry officer's uniform of the Indian Wars period.

homespun militia uniforms. Like Southern horses, the recruits themselves supplied the army with these uniforms, under the commutation system. After 1862, Southern quartermasters attempted to standardize the attire of the Confederate army, by commissioning uniforms for the enlisted men (officers still had to provide their own). The official cavalry uniform was made from the familiar gray or butternut woolen fabric, trimmed with yellow piping, with the trousers tucked into square-toed and heeled riding boots. But the Northern blockade meant that these materials soon ran short and a more piecemeal approach to uniforming the Confederacy prevailed.

Troops on both sides also wore captured uniforms, and the threadbare Confederate troops were often at least partly dressed in Union blue and Union boots. By the later stages of the conflict, it was often impossible to tell the different troops apart by only their dirty and tattered rags.

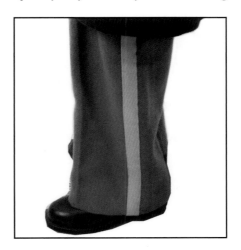

Left: Detail of the trousers with their distinctive yellow striping.

Below: Custer's favorite gun, a .50 caliber Remington single shot rifle. He wrote to the company to praise the gun.

Right: Pair of buffalo skin gloves for use during the bitter Plains winter.

In the postbellum era of the United States Cavalry, the force focused its attention on the American interior. Cavalry regiments stationed on the Frontier often adopted items of Western garb, in response to the prevailing conditions. The flamboyant General Custer and his officers (including his brother Tom Custer, and Captains Cook and Keogh) were famous for wearing an "undress" cavalry uniform of their own invention. This consisted of fringed buckskin jackets and trousers, buckskin gauntlets, broad-brimmed scouting hats, and long leather riding boots. The group was probably dressed like this when they perished at Custer's Last Stand. Many enlisted men bought their own shirts and neckerchiefs, carrying their standard issue dark blue blouses rolled up on their saddles. By the 1880s, the field uniform had somewhat adapted to the conditions of the West, but the dress uniform introduced in 1882 was extremely elaborate. Based on contemporary Prussian cavalry attire, it was festooned with braid, tassels, and gilt buttons. Needless to say, this was not designed for field use.

Civilian cavalry scouts, who were often Native Americans of the Seminole or Apache tribes, also had a kind of uniform. This was often a hybrid of the cavalry uniform (often the dark blue jacket) and native dress. Apaches in particular often wore a headband, and red was their favored color. In 1890, the cavalry authorized a special badge to be worn by their scouts; this consisted of crossed arrows in nickel, with

Right: Custer wearing his undress cavalry uniform of fringed buckskin.

red and white cords. Rank chevrons were also authorized for the Indian scouts.

Buckskin gloves became particularly popular with cavalrymen; they were soft and comfortable, while still offering good protection to the hands and wrists. They were often beaded, embroidered, or fringed. Native American craftsmen and women (particularly from the Nez Perce tribe) sold thousands of pairs of carefully crafted buckskin gloves to the cavalry.

FORT SMITH

✶   ✶   ✶   ✶   ✶   ✶

Military forts played a huge role in the settling and "taming" of the West and became symbols of safety and civilization to white Frontier settlers. They have also passed into Western folklore, movies, and literature.

Right: The Commissary at Fort Smith, where Judge Isaac Parker lodged for a while.

The origins of most Frontier forts dated back to the early part of the nineteenth century, and most were in use for the greater part of that century, changing their function as the turbulent history of those decades rolled out. Many forts also formed the nucleus of what started out as frontier settlements, and became the major towns and cities of today.

In many ways, the history and development of Fort Smith in Arkansas is fairly typical of this type of Frontier fort, and parallels the development of many similar establishments. But in addition to this, Fort Smith became critical in the enforcement of Frontier justice.

Built on the Arkansas River at the southern edge of the Ozarks, Fort Smith was the first frontier fort constructed in Arkansas. It was originally constructed in 1817, at the junction of the Poteau and Arkansas Rivers. The role of its garrison was to patrol Indian Territory, and to promote peace between the indigenous Osage and the in-coming Cherokee. Troops based at Fort Smith attempted to keep hunting disputes from flaring into outright war between the two tribes. John Rogers founded the town around the Fort in the 1820s. His smart brick house, built in the early 1840s, still stands at 400 North Eighth Street.

The first military fort on the site was abandoned in 1824, but the town of Fort Smith became an important staging post on the notorious "Trail of Tears." This was the route ordained for the forced removal of five native tribes (the Cherokees, Choctaws, Chickasaws, Creeks, and Seminoles) under the terms of the 1830 Indian Removal Act. This act decreed that these dispossessed tribes should be removed to the lands West of the Mississippi. Between 1830 and 1850, 100,000 Native Americans undertook the journey along the infamous Trail, and many perished. For the remainder of the century, Fort Smith reflected both the history of the nation and the U.S. government's turbulent Indian policy.

A second Fort Smith was begun in 1838 on a 306-acre plot bought for $15,000. It was completed in 1846 at a cost of $300,000. It became the "Motherpost of the Southwest," supplying military forts throughout the Southwest. In 1858, Fort Smith became a stop on the overland mail route that connected the East to the West.

Fort Smith began in the Civil War on the Confederate side, with two companies of the Confederate cavalry garrisoned at the military post, commanded by Captain Samuel Sturgis. At

Right: The confluence of the Arkansas and Poteau Rivers, where the original fort was built.

Left: A cameo portrait of Mrs. John Rogers.

Below: The plaque on the front of the Rogers' historic home, dating it from 1840.

the outbreak of war, Sturgis abandoned the position almost immediately, though Rebel cavalry units from Texas, Louisiana, and Arkansas soon reoccupied it. But when Federal troops reasserted their control of Indian Territory in 1863, Fort Smith came under intense pressure and fell to the Union on September 2, 1863. The Federal occupiers immediately reinforced the Fort Smith's defenses with rifle pits, trenches, and artillery emplacements. The town came under attack from Rebel troops on July 27, but these forces had given up the siege by early August. For the rest of the war, Fort Smith provided refuge to many, including former slaves fleeing the South, and frontier families dispossessed by the War. In February 1865, the townsfolk asked President Lincoln for emergency food and supplies.

After the war, the troops at Fort Smith became active participants in the Reconstruction of the South, controlling U.S. troops in Arkansas, Texas, and Indian Territory. In 1871,

the military post at Fort Smith was abandoned for a second time, and the Infantry troops finally withdrew in September that year.

In Fort Smith's post-military period, the settlement became an increasingly pivotal Frontier town. The federal district court for the Western District of Arkansas was relocated from Van Buren, Arkansas, to the Fort's refurbished officer's barracks in 1872.

Fort Smith's most famous citizen, "Hanging" Judge Isaac Parker, arrived in the town on May 4, 1875, and was to remain until his death. Parker was raised in Belmont County, Ohio, on the edge of the Frontier. Although he was brought up on a farm, Parker decided to become a lawyer, passing his bar exam in 1859. He became the city attorney of St. Joseph, Missouri in 1861, and was elected to Congress in 1871. Parker was particularly instrumental in supporting President Grant's Indian Appropriation Bill of 1872, and became

Left and Above:

The Rogers' home at 400 North Eighth Street, Fort Smith, still standing. John Rogers's cameo portrait, the other half of the pair with that of his wife, opposite.

Below: An early photograph of Judge Isaac Parker, aged 35.

known as "the Indians' best friend." This earned Parker the President's gratitude. When he lost his Congressional seat in 1874, Grant showed his appreciation by appointing Parker to the position of Federal District Judge for the Western District of Arkansas on March 18, 1875. The appointment was made under the terms of the Act to Establish the Judicial Courts of the United States.

The newly appointed Parker traveled to Fort Smith from Missouri on the steamboat Ella Hughes, and arrived in the town on May 4, 1875. On May 8, the *Fort Smith Herald* remarked, "We have met the Judge and were favorably impressed with his appearance—open and manly in expression, and apparently a sociable and affable gentlemen." Parker and his family took up residence in the stone commissary building of the Old Fort. At this time, Fort Smith had no paved streets, sidewalks, streetlights, factories, good hotels, or schools. The Judge described Indian Territory in

Left: The officers' quarters at the old fort became Fort Smith's courtroom, and the basement was converted into a jail.

Right: The interior of the courtroom, showing proceedings.

Below: Judge Parker's courtroom is preserved at the Fort Smith National Historic Site.

Right: A group of US Marshals photographed at Vinita, Oklahoma, after the fight with outlaw Ned Christie in November 1892.

his correspondence, saying, "the facilities for transport are meager and primitive. The country is sparsely settled." The town was also a focus of serious lawlessness, as the likes of the Daltons, Bill Powers, Dick Broadwell, Henry Starr, and Jim Reed walked its streets.

The end of the Civil War had unleashed a tide of racial violence and unchecked criminality. Many criminals moved west to Indian Territory, trying to outrun the law. They roamed the wild country, raping, murdering, and looting, with very little recourse from the authorities. The installation of Parker as the area's lone Federal Judge was designed to counterbalance this desperate state of anarchy. He went on to appoint two hundred United States Marshals to police an area of 74,000 square miles, sparsely inhabited by 60,000 people; sixty-five of these men eventually would lose their lives trying to impose the rule of law. Although Parker was salaried at $2,000 a year, the Marshals were only paid bounties and rewards.

It took Parker no time at all to earn his "Hanging" soubriquet. On September 3, 1875, six convicted men swung from the newly constructed Fort Smith gallows. During the Judge's tenure at the Fort Smith courthouse, he tried 13,490 cases, 344 of which were for

Left: A group of US Marshals in front of the old federal jail.

Right: Judge Parker's gallows at Fort Smith.

Left: A photographic portrait of hangman George Maledon.

Above: Maledon went about armed with two revolvers. Here is one of them, a Colt Frontier.

Below: The courtroom at Fort Smith was
extended to two stories in the late 1800s.

capital offences. Parker secured 9,454 convictions, and sentenced 160 men and women to hang, with 79 sentences actually being carried out in time. Parker's famous henchman, George Maledon ("the Prince of Hangmen"), hung sixty of these condemned criminals, and shot two more as they tried to escape justice. Parker's courtroom became the most famous in the West, and has been preserved for posterity. It was the scene of more judicial execution than any other place in American history.

Anna Davies, daughter of Senator Henry Davies, christened Parker's jail (originally located under the Fort Smith Courthouse) "Hell on the Border." This was during her 1885 trip around Indian Territory.

Parker's court retained a great deal of autonomous power until September 1896, when it was stripped of its authority over Indian Territory. This followed a national trend towards centralized authority, but seems to have been precipitated by the escape of Cherokee Bill from the Fort Smith jailhouse in the summer of 1895, during which a prison guard was killed.

Parker died a little over two months later, in November 1896, worn out from years of overwork. Despite his violent reputation, his obituary described him as "one of God's noblemen… (with) a great heart."

Fort Smith had several other famous residents, including

Frank Dalton, the law-abiding brother of the Dalton Gang members. He was appointed Fort Smith's Deputy Marshall in 1884, and was shot dead trying to arrest Dave Smith, a local horse thief.

Local brothel and saloonkeeper, Pearl Starr, also came from a notorious family. Her mother was the infamous bandit,

Above: Jail prisoners slept on the floor, with just a straw mattress and a single blanket.

Left: Interior of the jail, which was nicknamed "Hell on the Border."

Above: A prisoner's view through the bars of the jail, with the old Commissary in the distance.

Left: Cherokee Bill, who's real name was Crawford Goldsby.

Above: A lithograph of Cherokee Bill's hanging on March 17, 1896.
Below left: A studio portrait of Judge Isaac Parker.
Below: Pearl Starr, the daughter of Belle Starr. Pearl ran a notorious brothel in Fort Smith.

Left: Belle Starr and Blue Duck, her Native American husband.

Above: Blue Duck's Colt single action revolver.

Below: Fort Smith's Historic Site marker.

Belle Starr. Pearl became a prostitute after her mother's early demise in a shootout, but soon graduated to keeping her own bordello, identified with a bright red star surrounded by lighted pearls. Pearl boasted that her establishment had the most beautiful girls west of the Mississippi, piano music, and good liquor. The brothel was extremely successful, and Starr invested in several other Fort Smith businesses. She was finally run out of town in 1921, when the town authorities made prostitution illegal.

Fort Smith provided the setting and inspiration behind several famous Western movies and television films. These included *True Grit* (1969) starring John Wayne; *Hang 'Em High* (1968) starring Clint Eastwood; *Frank and Jesse* (1994) starring Bill Paxton and Rob Lowe; the Civil War miniseries *The Blue and the Gray* (1982); and *Lonesome Dove* (1989). The original location of the town's two military forts was designated a National Historic Site in 1960.

Fort's Smith population has now grown to 83,461. In honor of its great contribution to enforcing law and order on the West, the town is now the location of the United States Marshall's Service National Museum.

Stone Marker

This small square stone marker of 1858 marked the border between the United States and Indian Territory. On the top, it is engraved with the points of the compass, West being the territory of the Indian Nations. It is sited on the perimeter of Fort Smith's old fort on the bank of the Arkansas River.

GUNFIGHTERS OF THE OLD WEST

Commodore Owens was the "Law of the West"
When outlaws defied him, they went to their rest,
He carried a forty-four by each side,
When he went after outlaws, they surrendered or died."

John S. Fuller

Right: Dodge City's Main Street.

Of all the wild characters of the Frontier, the gunfighters were perhaps the most feared and flamboyant. They were not simply violent, for in a violent age, this was hardly unique. As the editor of the *Kansas City Journal* remarked in 1881, "The gentleman who has "killed his man" is by no means a *rara avis*… He is met daily on Main Street." The gunfighters whose reputations have survived all had some extra characteristic that has kept their image alive: high morals, depravity, good looks, mystery, vicious temper, sadism, marksmanship, or dandyism.

In fact the term "gunfighter" did not come into popular use until the 1870s. The earlier term was man-killer, or shootist (as bad man Clay Allison described himself). They were an integral part of the West, and a direct result of the conditions there. Whereas the law governed disputes in the East, the gun was the Western arbiter of choice. Gunfighters worked on both sides of the law, as both "civilizers" and criminals. Many swapped sides when it suited them. Most were motivated by money, and were only loyal to their own interests.

COMMODORE PERRY OWENS, 1852 - 1919

Commodore Owens was the "Law of the West"
When outlaws defied him, they went to their rest,
He carried a forty-four by each side,
When he went after outlaws, they surrendered or died."
John S. Fuller

Commodore Perry Owens (named for the famous naval commander) was a gunman who stood foursquare on the side of law and order. But his methods were rooted in the style of the Old West, and soon got him into trouble.

Owens ran away from his Tennessee home at the age of thirteen. Teased for his unusual name, he cultivated a famously flamboyant appearance, with waist-length strawberry-blonde hair, and a neatly trimmed moustache. He started out as a roping and branding cowboy, but also worked as a buffalo hunter, and for Wells Fargo. He was considered a dead shot, and became famous for his use of the cross-draw of the brace of pistols he wore at around his hips. The technique gave him a split-second advantage over his opponents. For tough jobs, he also carried a Winchester.

While working as a cattle foreman, Owens got into trouble for shooting a Navajo horse rustler. He was tried for the offence, but acquitted. His notoriety helped him to get elected as the sheriff of Apache County, Arizona, where he was responsible for over 21,000 square miles of lawless territory. His reputation for iron nerves ad brilliant horsemanship preceded him. During his time in the job as a single-handed law enforcer, Owens tamed the volatile town of Holbrook, shooting six members of the Snider Gang in the notorious Round Valley Gunfight. He also became involved in the Pleasant Valley War. This was a turf feud between families of cattle ranchers and sheep farmers. Under pressure to serve an arrest warrant on the horse rustler Andy Blevins (who also used the alias of "Cooper"), Sheriff Owens went out to the Blevins family ranch. Unfortunately, Cooper refused to come quietly, and a shootout ensued. Within a minute, Owens had fired five shots, four of which killed Cooper, Sam Blevins, and Mose Roberts, and wounded John Blevins. Owens would

Left: The Dodge City Peace Commission of 1883.

Right: Commodore Perry Owens poses with his rifle.

probably have been hailed as a hero, except that Sam Blevins was little more than a boy (although he had been armed and ready to kill the lawman). Sam's death turned the tide of public opinion against Owens, and an inquest ensued. Although he was acquitted of any blameworthy conduct, the *Saint Johns Herald* distilled the general mood, "the common people are beginning to think that our territory has had enough of desperadoes as 'peace' officers… [who] shoot whom they please."

Aggrieved by this treatment, Owens scrawled this message on the back of Andy Cooper's tombstone, "Party against whom this warrant was issued was killed while resisting arrest."

Owens was relieved of his commission, and the court officials attempted to withhold his outstanding pay until he took this from them at gunpoint. Leaving his steady job, Owens became a gun for hire on the side of law enforcement. For a time, he worked as a guard for the Atlantic and Pacific Railroad, but later returned to public service as a Deputy US Marshall.

WYATT EARP, 1848 - 1929

Wyatt Berry Stapp Earp was another famous gunslinger lawman, who enforced, upheld, and manipulated the law. He grew up on a farm in Iowa, but his family moved west to California in 1864. Wyatt soon found more "classic" Western employment, taking turns as a shotgun messenger for Wells Fargo, a buffalo hunter, a driver for Phineas Banning's Stage Line, and a railway employee. Later, he also mined for copper, gold, and silver and owned several saloons. Earp's weapon of choice was a Colt pistol, either an Army or a Peacemaker. He is also reputed to have carried a Colt "Buntline Special," with a detachable carbine. A complex and interesting personality, Earp was considered "a cold fish," ruthless, and decisive. Despite this, he was also a loyal friend who formed lifelong alliances with other famous gunfighters, such as Bat Masterson and Doc Holliday. Like them, he was also a compulsive gambler.

Earp returned east and married Urilla Sutherland in 1870. But his new wife died after just a few months of marriage. In 1875, Wyatt became marshal of the cattle town Wichita, Kansas, and gained something of a reputation in the town. His deputy, Jimmy Cairns described him. "Wyatt Earp was a wonderful officer. He was game to the last ditch and apparently afraid of nothing. The cowmen all respected

Above: Wyatt Earp, who fought in the most famous shoot-out of all time, at the O.K. Corral.

him and seemed to recognize his superiority and authority." In 1876, Earp became deputy marshal in 1876, and became acquainted with Bat Masterson. In 1879, Earp joined his brothers in the silver-mining boomtown of Tombstone, Arizona. In dress and manners, the Earps were notorious as quintessential Western gunmen, poised in manner and stylish in their dress. Earp's weapon of choice was a Colt pistol, either an Army or a Peacemaker. He is also reputed to have carried a Colt "Buntline Special" with a detachable carbine. The long barrel of this gun was useful for pistol-whipping cowboys, and disarming troublemakers.

Gradually, the Earps became established in Tombstone, and built up their assets. Wyatt acquired the gambling concession in the town's luxurious Oriental Saloon, and his brother Virgil became town marshal. Their brother Morgan also worked for

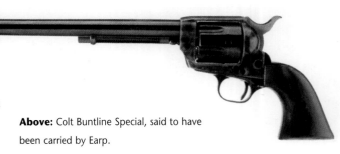

Above: Colt Buntline Special, said to have been carried by Earp.

the Tombstone police department. Wyatt also met his second wife, Josephine Marcus, in the town. But the Earps' life in Tombstone soon became difficult. A feud developed between them and the horse-thieving Clanton-McLaury. Their differences culminated in the most famous Western gunfight of all time, which took place in 1881 outside the O.K. Corral. Three Earp brothers survived, together with their supporter Bat Masterson, but Doc Holliday was wounded in the fight. Worse was to come. Virgil Earp was shot in the shoulder in December, and Morgan Earp was gunned down by an unknown assassin in the following year. The Earps took part in a spree of revenge killings, gunning down Florentino Cruz, Frank Stilwell, and "Curley Bill" Brocious. They were forced to ride out of Arizona Territory in 1882.

But Wyatt remained a law enforcer of sorts. In 1893, he became a member of the eight-man strong "Dodge City Peace Commission," in company with Bat Masterson, Luke Short, W.H. Harris, Frank McLain, W.F Petillon, Neal Brown, and Charlie Bassett. The town's corrupt officials wanted to close down Luke Short's saloon as part of a town clean-up. Short's friends came to town to support his cause, and were sworn in as deputy marshals by constable "Prairie Dog" Dave Marrow. The town officials backed down pretty quickly.

Wyatt and Josie spent the next few years tramping around booming Frontier mining towns, gambling, and investing in saloons and real estate. In 1897 they opened a saloon in Nome, Alaska, at the peak of the northern gold rush, and made a fortune estimated at $80,000. The Earps then head for Tonopah, Nevada, cashing-in on the town's gold strike. Ultimately, Earp took up prospecting himself, and staked several claims in the Mojave Desert, including several just outside Death Valley. It was rumored that he managed to off-load a worked-out silver mine for $30,000. He struck gold and copper in 1906, and spent the final winters of his life working these veins. He and Josie lived in Los Angeles in the summer, and mixed with the Hollywood glitterati. John Wayne claimed to have met Earp when he was working as a stagehand and extra, and said that he used Earp's manner as inspiration for his gun-slinging characters.

Wyatt died in Lost Angeles in 1929, at the age of 80. He was one of a very few Western gunfighters to make it to old age, and perhaps unique in that he was able to enjoy his own burgeoning reputation. Like all the Western shootists, Earp has his own tricks of the trade. He claimed that he only ever loaded five bullets into a six-shooter to "ensure against accidental discharge."

JOHN "DOC" HOLLIDAY, 1851 – 1887

"Holliday has a big reputation as a fighter, and has probably put more rustlers and cowboys under the sod than any other man in the west. He had been the terror of the lawless element in Arizona, and with the Earps was the only man brave enough to face the bloodthirsty crowd which has made the name of Arizona a stench in the nostrils of decent men."
The Denver Republican, May 22, 1882

"Doc Holliday was afraid of nothing on earth."
Bat Masterson

Above: John "Doc" Holliday, who began his professional life as a dentist in Dodge City.

John "Doc" Holliday was unusual amongst the gunfighters of the west in that he came from a well-to-do background. He was born in Griffin, Georgia, to Henry Burroughs Holliday and Alice Jane Holliday, and was their eldest surviving child. Henry Burroughs Holliday was a Confederate Major in the Civil War, a wealthy planter and lawyer, who was later elected Major of Valdosa, Georgia. But misfortune came quickly. John was intensely close to his mother, but she died in 1866. To compound his loss, his father remarried within an indecently hasty three months.

Soon after he gained his degree qualifying him as a Doctor

in Dental Surgery from the Pennsylvania College of Dental Surgery in Philadelphia, a second blow fell. He was diagnosed with tuberculosis. Told he had only months with live, Holliday spent the balance of his life on borrowed time, and this may have accounted for the extremely cavalier way in which he led it.

The "Doc" had begun to practice dentistry in various Western boomtowns, including Dodge City, but his illness necessitated a move west to a hotter, drier climate. By now, Holliday was too ill to follow his profession, as terrible coughing spells wracked his frame, so he headed to Dallas. Like so many men of his type, he became a professional gambler. Fellow gunman, and unequivocal good guy, Bat Masterson, later described Holliday as being of a "mean disposition and an ungovernable temper, and under the influence of liquor… a most dangerous man." Perhaps at least some of this ill humor was due to his impending doom. His unpleasant temper and vagabond lifestyle resulted in a corrosive cocktail of violence and murder. Holliday went about armed with a gun in a shoulder holster, a gun on his

face ad neck, and almost removed his head. At this time, he also became involved with the only woman that ever came into his life, Big Nose Kate. Big Nose was a successful madam and prostitute who worked in these professions by choice. She was also one of the most famous of the gunwomen of the West, and an excellent shot. Although she and Doc attempted to live together respectably, the bright saloon lights were her natural habitat, and she returned to them time after time. On and off, their volatile relationship lasted for many years. On one occasion, Big Nose sprang Doc from jail in Fort Griffin, but when their relationship soured, she just as quickly turned him in to the Law.

The pattern of Doc's life was now set. Effectively, he was a professional man-killer. He rode with Wyatt Earp for some time, adding to his murder tally. In Earp's company, he became a member of the Dodge City Peace Commission, and was present at the O.K. Corral shootout. Indeed, one of Holliday's few redeeming features was his deep sense of loyalty to his friends, and to Earp in particular. Earp described his friend as a "most skilful gambler, and the nerviest, fastest, deadliest man with a six-gun I ever saw." But although Wyatt valued Holliday's loyalty and gun skills, he was also embarrassed by his behaviour.

Although Doc claimed he had escaped nine attempts on his life, including five ambushes and four hangings, he finally died in bed in Glenwood Springs, Colorado. His failing health had led him to this health resort to try the sulphur spring water. He was just thirty-six years old, but contemporary accounts described his body as being so ravaged by drink and illness that he looked like a man of eighty. He took to his bed for fifty-seven days, and was delirious for fourteen of them. Considering his style of life, this was a very strange way for him to die. His final words referred to this. "This is funny," he said.

ROBERT CLAY ALLISON, "THE SHOOTIST," 1840 – 1887

Robert Clay Allison was no gentleman gunfighter. Like Doc Holliday, he was a moody and vicious man who bred fear in all who knew him. Unlike him, he had no friends. Allison was born in Tennessee, and joined the Confederate Army at the beginning of the Civil War. But he was soon discharged due to "personality problems." His discharge papers

hip and a long, wicked knife. His long list of killings started with the murder of a local gambler in Dallas, and a pattern of "kill and run" established itself so that Doc never felt safe in any one place for too long. The most foolish murder he committed was that of a soldier from Fort Richardson, which brought him to the attention of the US Government. Doc escaped, but now had a price on his head, and was wanted by the Army, a selection of US Marshals, Texas Rangers, and local lawmen. He moved to Denver, remaining almost anonymous until he slashed a gambler, Bud Ryan, across the

Above: Robert Clay Allison is shown with his leg in plaster, having discharged his own gun before he drew.

Above: A more conventional portrait of Allison as a younger man. He was killed when his own wagon ran him over.

described him as "incapable of performing the duties of a soldier because of a blow received many years ago. Emotional or physical excitement produces paroxysmals [sic.] of a mixed character, partly epileptic and partly maniacal." Allison worked as a trail hand after leaving the army, and moved to the Texan Brazos River Territory in 1865, driving cattle to New Mexico. Things obviously went well for him, as by 1870, he had acquired his own ranch in Colfax County, New Mexico. But local newspapers were already reporting that he had despatched as many as fifteen men, and he had a grim reputation for violence, especially when he was drunk.

His first truly notorious, and grotesque, killing happened in late 1870. Allison was drinking in a saloon when a hysterical woman approached him. She told him that her husband had gone mad and killed a number of his own ranch hands at their cabin, together with their own infant daughter. Allison rounded up a posse, but they found no bodies at the ranch. However, a few days later, bones were discovered on the property, and the ranch owner was arrested and imprisoned. Enraged by the man's behaviour, Allison broke him out of jail, lynched him, and cut off his head, riding twenty-nine miles to Cimmaron with this gruesome trophy on a pole, before displaying the head in a local saloon. This kind of depraved behaviour did nothing to endear people to Allison, who was clearly mad. His presence also attracted other man-killers to the area, who wanted to enhance their own reputations by adding him to their list of kills. Chunk Colbert coolly invited Allison out to dinner, before trying to shoot him under the table. Fortunately for him, Allison beat him to it, just as coffee was served. When he was asked why he had accepted a dinner invitation from a man he knew was out to kill him, Allison responded that he "didn't want to send a man to hell on an empty stomach."

His behaviour became increasingly deranged. When a dental appointment to cure a raging toothache went awry, and the nervous dentist began to drill the wrong tooth, Allison furiously bundled him into his own chair and ripped off half the man's lip in a botched effort to extract one of the dentist's own teeth.

Another event that demonstrates Allison's bizarre view of the world is the Bowie knife grave affair. He had fallen into dispute with a neighboring rancher, and suggested that they should settle their differences by digging a grave big enough to hold them both. They should then climb into the pit; each armed only with a Bowie knife. The survivor could them climb out. It was also agreed that the victor would arrange a tombstone for the vanquished. But events overtook Allison, and this encounter never took place. Driving supplies back from Pecos, Texas, he fell from the wagon, and one of the wheels ran over his neck, killing him instantly.

This rather ignominious end was unusual for a shootist of this period. Men of Allison's type generally expired in a hail of bullets, or dancing at the end of a rope.

JESSE WOODSON JAMES, 1847 – 1882

Jesse was born in Clay County, Missouri, a younger brother by four years to Frank James, whom he came to dominate throughout his life. Jesse fought, notionally, on the Confederate side during the Civil War, but was actually embroiled in a parallel guerrilla campaign. This consisted of raiding, stealing, and murdering civilians, although his commander noted that he was the "keenest…fighter in the command." This violent period formed Jesse's outlook for life. His father, Robert James (a Baptist minister), had been murdered by Kansas raiders; and his formidable mother, Zerelda James Samuel was imprisoned for spying against the Union. He himself had been badly wounded in a shootout with a party of Union cavalry. This all led to an enduring hatred of everything that reminded him of authority, and the "oppressive" North. Strangely, this included banks and trains. When he returned home from the War, Jesse formed a family gang of outlaws, which included his brother Frank and four younger half-brothers.

Above: An early photograph of Jesse James. His gang initiated a sixteen-year murder spree.

As they initially confined their attacks to the aforementioned banks and trains, the James Gang had some public support. This was in spite of the fact that they often killed innocent bystanders during their raids, including a schoolboy. John Newman Edwards, the famous Missouri editor, referred to Jesse as "America's Robin Hood" who adhered to a "chivalry of crime."

Perhaps the James Gang's most enduring claim to fame is that it invented the bank robbery, and also staged the first large-scale train hold-up in the country's history. James played along with his public image, handing a press release

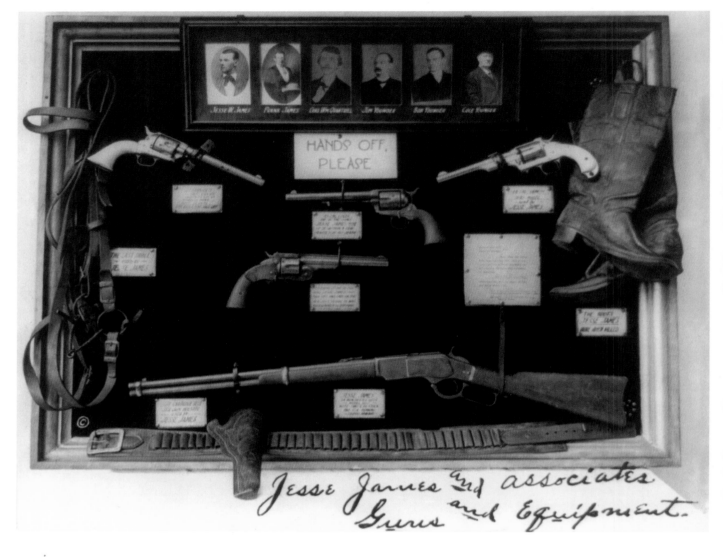

Above: A collection of equipment owned by Jesse James and his gang, the "Outlaws."

to the conductor of a train the gang had just raided. This document helpfully described their attack as the "Most Daring Robbery on Record." Considerately, James left a blank space for the value of their spoils. The banks finally grew tired of the gang's activities, and hired the Pinkerton Detective Agency to track down the gang. But despite the Pinkertons' motto, "We Never Sleep," The James Gang murdered several agents who tried to infiltrate their territory. In 1875, he frustrated Pinks finally mounted a grenade attack on the James' family home. Their strategy disastrously backfired. Frank and Jesse's nine-year-old half brother was killed in the raid, and their mother's arm was so badly shattered that it had to be amputated. Frank and Jesse got away.

The agency was roundly condemned for this barbaric behavior, and the public outcry was so great that the James Gang were almost awarded amnesty.

The Gang continued their spree of thieving and murder until the tables were finally turned on them in 1876. They attempted to hold up the First National Bank in Northfield, Minnesota, but the bank staff and several townspeople retaliated. A massive gun battle ensued. Three members of the gang were shot down, and three of the James brothers were captured. Frank and Jesse escaped, but Missouri Governor Thomas Crittenden offered rewards of $10,000 (reputedly on the advice of Allan Pinkerton) for turning in either Frank or Jesse. Pressure tightened on the brothers, and the threat of betrayal hung around their necks like millstones.

Jesse hardly ever took off his guns, and never turned his back to a door or window if he could help it.

Ultimately, it was the reward led to Jesse's betrayal. Gang members Robert and Charley Ford gunned him down in his own St. Joseph home. He had very unwisely put down his gun, just for a moment, to adjust a crooked picture. But the Fords were also betrayed, forced to share the reward with several officials, including Governor Crittenden, and were shunned and ridiculed as back-shooting cowards. Charley Ford couldn't stand this treatment, and committed suicide. Robert was condemned to the even worse fate of re-enacting the shooting every night in a stage show, where he was often booed off stage. He was finally shot to death in a tent saloon in Creede, Colorado.

> It was on Saturday night, Jesse was at home
> Talking to his family brave
> Robert Ford came along like a thief in the night
> And laid poor Jesse in his grave.
>
> It was Robert Ford, that dirty little coward
> I wonder how he does feel
> For he ate of Jesse's bread and he slept in Jesse's bed
> Then laid poor Jesse in his grave.

Jesse's vicious campaign of murder and pillage, which had lasted for sixteen years, was finally over. His death concluded one of the most serious crime waves ever to hit the West.

In a strange footnote to his story, Jesse's rather bizarre and fiercely protective mother insisted that he was buried in the yard of the family home. She charged visitors 25 cents to see his tombstone, which read:

> Jesse W. James
> Died 3 April 1882
> Aged 34 years, 6 months, 28 days
> Murdered by a traitor and a coward whose name
> Is not worthy to appear here.

After Jesse's death, Frank James could no longer stand his claustrophobic life on the run. He turned himself in, saying, "I am tired of this life of taut nerves, of night-riding, and day-hiding… tired of seeing Judas on the face of every friend I know." N.C. Wyeth brought this paranoid tension to life in his epic portrait of the James gang in hiding: tension is etched into each face; each man nervously holds his gun. A

strangely sympathetic Missouri jury refused to convict the bereaved Frank, and he gave up his life of crime, spending the rest of his life in various humdrum jobs.

Even during their lifetime, the James gang was the subject of many dime novels, and their personality cult escalated after Jesse's death. There were many post mortem sightings of him, just as there would be for Elvis Presley in the twentieth century. But his death also signaled the end of the era of the bad man. Better methods of law enforcement meant that outlaws felt more and more exposed, and were forced to live in uncongenial and remote hideouts to escape detection.

HENRY MCCARTHY ANTRIM, ALIAS BILLY THE KID, 1859 – 1881

> I'll sing you a true song of Billy the Kid
> I'll sing of the desperate deeds that he did
> Way out in New Mexico long, long ago
> When a man's only chance was his own forty-four.
>
> When Billy the Kid was a very young lad
> In the old Silver City he went to the bad
> Way out in the West with a gun in his hand
> At the age of twelve years he killed his first man
>
> Now this is how Billy the Kid met his fate
> The bright moon was shining, the hour was late
> Shot down by Pat Garrett, who once was his friend,
> The young outlaw's life had now come to its end.

Billy The Kid, the teenage outlaw, was one of the most colorful figures of the Old West. He was a controversial figure both in life and in death. He is considered by some observers to be a cold-blooded, psychopathic killer, while others see him as boy who "loved his mother devotedly" and was led on by adults to a life of criminality. Even so, in both versions of his life story, he is credited with at least six killings, though his ballad claims that, actually "He'd a notch on his pistol for twenty-one men."

Billy was born on New York's East Side in November 1859. His father died when he and his brother Joseph were very young. His mother, Catherine, died in 1874, just a year after remarrying. By this time, the family was in Silver City, New Mexico, where they had gone to seek a cure for their mother's tuberculosis. Billy's stepfather didn't want the two boys, so he put them into foster homes where The Kid had to wash

Left: A tin type photograph of Billy the Kid, alias Henry McCarthy Antrim.

Below: The Maxwell House where Billy the Kid was shot in July 1881.

Above: Pat Garrett who pulled the trigger on Billy the Kid. He was promoted to the office of sheriff of Lincoln County.

dishes to earn his keep.

Billy's juvenile life of crime started at this time. He stole some butter from a rancher, and went on to steal laundry. Unfortunately, being locked up for this minor misdemeanor scared him so much that he decided to escape up the chimney. For the next couple of years, he tramped around working as a ranch hand and gambler, trying to avoid brushes with the law. But everything went down hill rapidly after he shot and killed a bully who was teasing him. Now unable to get honest work, he reluctantly joined a gang of rustlers known as "The Boys."

Involvement with these criminals was pretty distasteful to him, so Billy got legitimate work with English rancher John Tunstall. Determined the change everything in his life, the Kid assumed a new alias, William H. Bonney. Many believe that Billy looked upon his employer as the father he had lost, and that he tried to reform his character for Tunstall's sake. Unfortunately, John Tunstall was murdered, and his killing sparked the Lincoln County War. When this violent feud finally wound up, The Kid's involvement on the side of the Regulators (who were responsible for at least two murders) meant that he had once more fallen afoul of the law. He was now unable to find lawful employment, so he drifted into gambling and cattle rustling. Knowing that the new Governor of the territory, Lew Wallace, wanted to re-establish order in Lincoln County, The Kid turned himself in. He offered to turn state's evidence against other participants in the hostilities of the Lincoln County War, and Governor Wallace accepted. But when he realized that the court was loaded against him, Billy decided to escape once more.

By now, he was a celebrity, and his activities were widely reported in the newspapers, who coined his soubriquet "Billy The Kid." The Kid was reputedly fed up with having every murder in the West attributed to him, but admitted "I don't know, as if anyone would believe anything good of me." For two years, The Kid managed to avoid capture, but when he was framed for the murder of deputy James Carlyle, Pat Garrett was charged with bringing him in. Garrett finally caught up with The Kid on December 23, 1880, in a cabin in Stinkpot Springs. After a brief standoff, Billy surrendered. He was charged and sentenced for the murder of Sheriff Brady during the Lincoln County War, and was taken back to Lincoln to await hanging. The Kid was fully aware that there could now be no reprieve so he made his final escape, killing guard J.W. Bell, and taking time out to gun down Robert Olinger, who had bated him with his own shotgun during his

Right: The Condon
Bank at Coffeyville,
Kansas. The bank was
the Dalton gang's
second target in their
raid on their
hometown.

Above: An unusual panoramic photograph of Coffeyville, Kansas, taken after it received notoriety in the wake of the Daltons' infamy.

Below: The ignominious end of the Dalton gang. The corpses of Brat and Bob Dalton, Bill Powers, and Dick Broadwell were laid out outside the Coffeyville jail on October 5, 1892.

stay in prison. The Kid reckoned that he wouldn't have shot Bell, except for the fact that he tried to run, but he offered no apology for Olinger's despatch.

Public opinion now swung against the Kid, and Pat Garrett was charged, once again, with bringing the youth to justice. It took Garrett three months to catch up with Billy in Fort Sumner, New Mexico. At the very moment that Garrett was pumping rooming house owner Pete Maxwell for intelligence about the Kid's movements, Billy walked in to get a steak for dinner. Garrett felled the youngster with two bullets from his .45 caliber, single-action Colt, one of which lodged in his heart. The Kid spoke fluent Spanish, and his rather pathetic final words were "Quién es? Quién es?" "Who is it? Who is it?"

Fair Mexican maidens play guitars and sing
A song about Billy, their boy bandit king

Billy's brief but colorful career as a gunman and outlaw was over. He was reputed to have gambled with Doc Holliday, dined with Jesse James, and gone target-shooting with Bat Masterson. But his advice to those that would follow in his

footsteps was simple. "Advise persons never to engage in killing." Many of his friends and acquaintances mourned his passing very sincerely, praising his sense of humor, his loyalty to his friends, his extreme bravery, and the kindness he showed his horses. The Kid looks a little simple in his portrait, but people spoke of his intelligence and cunning. Many also spoke derisively of Pat Garrett's self-interest. He gained the office of sheriff of Lincoln County for his work in killing The Kid, and cashed in by writing the best-selling biography, *The Authentic Life of Billy the Kid: The noted desperado of the Southwest*.

Billy was certainly no "good bad man." By the time of his death, he was pretty well bad through and through, and a casual murderer. But the teenage outlaw of the Southwest has left probably the biggest legend of any gunslinging wrongdoer of the West, fueling a huge tourist industry.

THE DALTON GANG

Lewis and Adeline Dalton had a large family of fifteen children: ten boys and five girls. Most were born in Cass County, Michigan, where Lewis owned a saloon, but the family later settled on a farm outside of Coffeyville, Kansas. With no hint of what was to come, the eldest son, Frank, became a Deputy US Marshal, working in the dangerous Indian Territory. His younger brothers revered him, and the whole family was devastated when he was cruelly murdered. His younger brothers, Emmett, Gratton, and Bob followed him into the service, but were soon disillusioned. Emmett described the work that was expected of them, "Grafting we of today know the term was a mild, soothing description of what occurred." There was also some disagreement over unpaid expenses, and the brothers quit. They subsequently became involved in a little cattle-rustling, and became outlaws, swapping to the wrong side of the law. This is a recurring pattern in the history of Western law enforcement.

The brothers began a brief but flashy career of robberies and hold-ups, and recruited other gang members, including George "Bittercreek" Newcomb, and Blackfaced Charlie Bryant. They planned to break all criminal records by pulling off a double-bank hoist in their hometown of Coffeyville. Choosing their hometown for the heist was their first and greatest mistake. The gang rode into town, armed with pearl handled Colt .45s, disguised as a US Marshal and his posse. But the Dalton brothers were almost instantly recognized by a passerby, who alerted the real Marshal and townsfolk.

The Daltons had planned to rob the First National Bank first, and then go on to the Condon Bank. The first raid went off successfully, but as they left the Condon Bank, the gang was met by a hail of bullets from a group of armed citizens, led by Marshal Charles T. Connelly. A massive gun battle ensued, in which Connelly and three townspeople were killed. After Connelly's demise, liveryman John J. Kloeher took over the attack and four members of the Dalton gang now fell, fatally shot in what became known as Death Alley. These were Bob and Gratton Dalton, Bill Powers, and Dick Broadwell. The youngest Dalton brother, Emmett was very seriously wounded, but he survived. The bodies of the dead gang members were treated with scant regard, photographed like trophies, and put on public display. For years, the gang members lay in a grave unmarked, except for a rusty piece of iron pipe to which the gang had tethered their horses. Emmett erected a headstone some years later. He himself served fourteen years in the Kansas State Penitentiary. On his release he went on to lead a blameless life. In 1909, Emmett was employed as a consultant on a movie of the Dalton Gang's last stand, and wrote several books condemning criminality. He died in 1937.

JAMES BUTLER "WILD BILL" HICKOK, 1837 – 1876

To this day, the reputation of Wild Bill Hickok epitomizes that of the gun fighting lawman. He was a genuine lover of law and order, as well as a great showman and latter day duelist.

Hickok was born in Troy Grove, Illinois, in 1837. He moved to Kansas in 1855, and was the town constable before reaching the age of 21. His career almost ended before it began when he inadvertently shot an unarmed man in his first killing. He was a contract scout, spy, and detective for the Union Army in the Civil War, and won the "Wild Bill" epithet during this time. His reputation grew, and in 1871, the citizens of Abilene finally asked him to be their town marshal. Most of his predecessors in the job lay in Boot Hill cemetery. They included the previous incumbent, pacifist Marshal Tom "Bear River" Smith, who had been murdered by an axe-wielding homesteader. Not unreasonably, the weary citizens of the town felt that a more intimidating individual would stand a better chance of keeping the peace, particularly during the annual spring cattle drives. These generally resulted in the town being completely torn up by lawless cowboys. In fact, Hickok's reputation wasn't entirely deserved. He was a tremendous self-publicist who actively propagated the fiction that he had killed over a hundred white men. His actual tally was closer to ten.

Hickok had worked as a scout during the Civil and Indian Wars, and had been elected sheriff of Hays County in 1869, but it was his reputation for dealing with frontier desperados that attracted the citizens of Abilene. Once installed as town marshal, he proceeded to clean up the town, running Abilene from a card table in the Long Branch Saloon, and earning a massive $150 a month for his services. One cowboy described him as looking like a "mad old bull" and he made every attempt to look as intimidating as possible. His habitual costume was a black frock coat, a low-brimmed black hat, and two ivory-butted and silver-mounted pistols thrust behind a red silk sash. In fact, the pistol handles were worn reversed to speed his draw. Hickok's larger-than-life presence kept a lid on much of the town violence.

He was also surprisingly successful in bringing gun control to the town, disarming even reluctant Texans. Hickok posted a notice that disarmament would be vigorously enforced, as reported by the *Abilene Chronicle*. Their editorial comment read, "There's no bravery in a carrying revolvers in a civilized community. Such a practice is well enough and perhaps necessary when among Indians or other barbarians, but among white people it ought to be discountenanced."

As marshal, Hickok was also responsible for street-cleaning, and kept the town roads clear of dead dogs and horses. He was also paid 50 cents for every stray dog he shot. On one occasion, he was called upon to dispatch a mad Texas longhorn that was rampaging through the town. Hickok greatly enjoyed his time in Abilene, rooming with a succession of prostitutes, gambling, and drinking heavily. The famous painter N.C. Wyeth painted a wonderfully atmospheric portrait of a dandified Hickok unmasking a card cheat in typical form. But his tenure in the cow town came to a disastrous end, when his deputy, Mike Williams, was killed in cross fire during a gunfight between Hickok and gambler Phil Coe. Hickok was devastated by Williams's death, weeping copiously as he laid his body on a snooker table in the saloon. He even paid for the deputy's funeral. After eight months of Hickok's "cleanup" Abilene's town council decided not to renew his expensive contract, and banned the cattle drives instead.

Jobless, Hickok drifted east, touring in a melodrama staged by Buffalo Bill, *The Scouts of the Plains*. But he was hopeless in his starring role. By this time, he was an unsteady drunk, and had a surprisingly high, girlish voice. He often threatened to shoot the stagehands. Broke, he drifted to Deadwood, trying to disguise his failing eyesight. A gold mining venture failed, so he returned to his old profession at the poker tables. He had always loved gambling, and had owned a couple of gambling joints at one time or other, in Junction City and Hays City. Gambling was how he met his end, shot in the back by the cowardly Jack McCall, who wanted a share of Hickok's reputation. As he fell, his hand of cards scattered across the table: the ace of spaces, the ace of clubs, the eight of clubs, the eight of spades, and the queen or jack of diamonds. To this day, this is know as the "dead man's hand."

His obituary in the *Cheyenne Daily Leader* was scathing. It implied that Hickok was an obsolete figure from the "lawless times" of the past, and that he had degenerated into a "tame and worthless loafer," his constitution ruined by "wine and women." But his Deadwood grave is visited to this day, and his legend is undiminished. Any gunman would have done well to listen to his professional advice, given in an interview of 1865, "Take time. I've known many a feller slip up for shootin' in a hurry." He maintained that he valued accuracy rather than speed, but then he was one of the fastest draws ever known in the West.

Above: Wild Bill Hickok was a "genuine lover of law and order."

GUNS OF THE WILD WEST

✷   ✷   ✷   ✷   ✷   ✷

The fallout from the Civil War had a significant impact on the development of the Western Frontier. Many men, who had learned the use of weapons in five years of bitter conflict, were now turned loose to colonize the new territories.

Gun design and technology had developed rapidly in the Civil War years. Troops who had begun the conflict with muzzle-loading, single-shot weapons, had ended up armed with repeating, breech-loading arms. These very weapons were in the hands of both the lawmen and the lawless. This made the West a volatile place and launched a particularly violent period in American history. The image portrayed by Hollywood may have made it seem that every Westerner was uniformly equipped with a Colt revolver and a Winchester rifle, but the reality was very different. The products of both these makers were expensive. The Colt Peacemaker of 1873 cost $17, which was a whole chunk of a month's wages for the average cowhand. A more affordable handgun would have been an army-issue Colt Navy, a Whitney, or a Remington. The Frontier was flooded with pistols like these in the post-War period. The same rationale was true for rifles. The new Winchester 1866 "Yellow Boy" carbine cost $40, which was equivalent to a whole month's wages for most men on the Frontier. An ex-Union Army Spencer Model 1860 was a far more sensible option. Concealed weapons, such as pocket pistols and derringers also became popular with many Westerners, particularly gamblers.

Of course, it could be argued that the right gun could save your life in the unstable Frontier, and was a good investment. But many were forced to arm themselves as best they could.

This section examines a wide variety of interesting weapons that saw action on the Frontier, particularly in the wild years between 1860 and the end of the century.

Right: Members of the Medicine Lodge citizens' posse, with their Winchester rifles.

COLT REVOLVERS

Samuel Colt's revolvers had proved popular in the Mexican War, as the government had wisely placed an order (instigated by Samuel Walker), for Colt's monster Model 1847, also known as the Colt Dragoon, or Colt Walker. Right from the start, Samuel Colt understood the significance of his guns to the Western market. Scenes of Dragoons fighting Indians, and other western combat, were engraved on the cylinders to illustrate this connection. Colt's percussion revolvers fought through the Civil War, and the post-War period. In 1873, the Single Action "Peacemaker" (as the gun was nicknamed) replaced these weapons. Along with the Winchester 1873 rifle, the Peacemaker can truthfully be said to have been one of the weapons "that won the West." Other handguns made appearances at gunfights, stage hold-ups, gambling dens, and along the dusty trails. But no other pistol eclipsed the reputation of the Colt.

1 First Model Dragoon made in 1848. This gun had a six-shot cylinder in .44 caliber, a 7½ inch barrel, and weighed a massive 4 pounds, 9 ounces.

2 Third Model Dragoon, identified by its rounded trigger guard and 8-inch barrel. 10,000 of these weapons were made between 1851 and 1860.

3 Model 1848 Baby Dragoon. This was made for the civilian market, which demanded lighter, less cumbersome weapons. It was a 5-shot .31-caliber weapon with optional barrel lengths. This one has a 5-inch barrel.

4 Model 1849 Pocket Revolver, which replaced the Baby Dragoon. Over 325,000 of this type were made between 1850 and 1873. The gun was available with 3-, 4-, 5-, or 6-inch barrels. This example has the popular 4-inch barrel.

5 Model 1849 Pocket Revolver in nickel finish, also with a 4-inch barrel. Both examples carry the address "Saml. Colt, New York City."

6 Model 1849 with Cartridge conversion. One of many examples of the model that were either new builds, or conversions, this gun has a new round barrel with no ejector, and is fitted with a new rebated cylinder, chambered for .38 centerfire cartridges. This gun remained in manufacture until 1880.

7 Colt Model 1849 Wells Fargo. This gun was a special order of weapons for the Wells Fargo company, designed to provide backup firepower for coach guards once they had used up their two shotgun rounds.

8 Model Navy 1851. This is an example of one of the most popular handguns ever made and is easily identified by its octagonal barrel. Over 215,000 were made between 1850 and 1873. The term "Navy" was eventually used to classify any revolver of .36 caliber. Many fighting men preferred the lighter weight of the Navy to other, heavier weapons. This model was available both for military and civilian order procurement.

9 Model 1860 Army. This was the .44 caliber equivalent of the "Navy." Designed to replace the Third Model Dragoon, over 127,000 of the total production run of 200,000 guns were procured by the U.S. Government. The gun weighed 2.74 pounds and had a 7.5- or 8-inch barrel.

10 Model 1861 Navy. This gun is distinguished by its rounded-off barrel and trigger guard. Over 39,000 examples of the weapon were produced.

11 The Colt-Richards. The conversion involved removing the ramming lever, turning off the rear of the cylinder, and adding a conversion plate to take rimmed cartridges, which were loaded and removed from the rear. This is a converted Model 1860 Army revolver.

12 Model 1862 Police revolver in .36 caliber. Over 28,000 examples of this model were made between 1861 and 1873. Many were employed as civilian weapons. This example has a 5½-inch barrel, and a 5-round fluted cylinder.

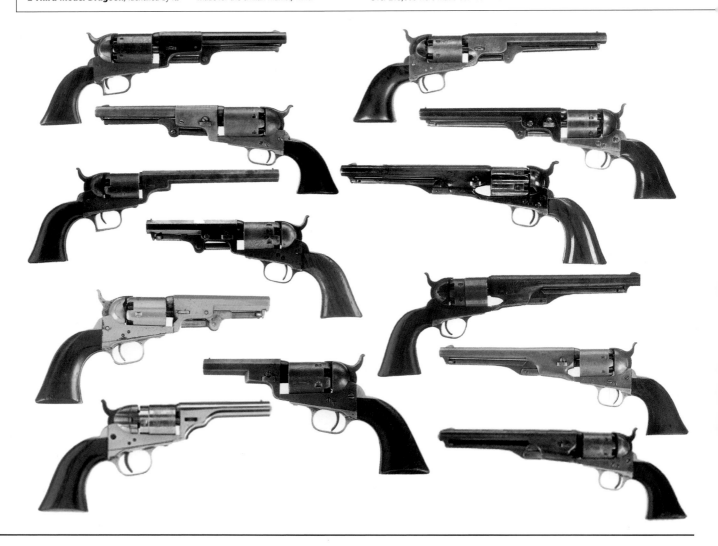

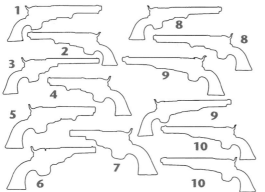

13 The Colt-Thuer Conversion. This conversion enabled Colt to circumvent the Rollin White patent on bored-through cylinders. The patent didn't expire until 1869. However, the conversion was a rather cumbersome affair, as the cartridges were still loaded and removed from the front.

14 Model 1873 Single Action. Another gun credited with being the "gun that won the West." It shared its .45 caliber with the Winchester 1873, and used the same ammunition. This meant that an individual only needed to carry a single type of cartridge in his saddlebag or belt. This example is heavily engraved by specialist engraver L.D. Nimschke. It also has added pearl grips.

15 Colt Storekeeper was a cut-down, lighter caliber version of the Lightening Model, which was developed for self-defence and easy concealment. It had a 3.5-inch barrel, and was .38 caliber.

16 Model 1873 with holster. This gun is .44 special caliber, and has a 4.75-inch barrel. The model was used by the legendary Arvo

Ojala to teach shooting and fast draw techniques to stars such as Clint Eastwood. It has certainly appeared on screen.

17 Model 1877 Lightning. This gun was essentially a slightly scaled down version of the Colt Army. It also had a double action to keep up with its competitors from manufacturers like Smith and Wesson. There were two versions: the Lightning in .38 caliber, and the .41 caliber Thunderer. Both new guns were recognizable by the bird's-

head-shaped butt. The weapon was popular with gunfighters, such as John Wesley Hardin, who owned an example.

18 Buntline Special. Legend places this type of gun in the hands of the Dodge City Peace Commission, which included Wyatt Earp. The guns were thoughtfully ordered by dime novelist Ned Buntline, whose real name was Edward Judson. In reality the gun (an adaptation of the single action), would not have been ideal for fast shooting. This was

due to the time it would have taken to clear the 12-inch barrels from a holster.

19 Model Frontier 1878. This weapon was used in the capture of Butch Cassidy. The gun is .44 caliber, double-action weapon, with a 4-inch barrel. It is an improved version of the Lightning. It is marked "J.H. Ward, Sheriff, Vinta, Colorado" on the backstrap.

COLT'S COMPETITORS

1 Beaumont Adams percussion revolver. Thousands of these guns were imported into the United States during the Civil War, by both sides. The gun was advanced for its time, being self-cocking. This gave the user double-action quick-fire in a fight at close-quarters. This example is in .44 caliber, with a 6-inch barrel.

2 Brooklyn Bridge Colt Copy. This is a classic example of the many copies that were made of the Colt Pocket models. It even has a battle engraving on the cylinder.

3 Cooper Pocket Revolver is one of around 15,000 made at the company's Philadelphia factory in the 1860's. An early double-action, .31 caliber gun, it would have been useful as a self-protection weapon.

4 Hopkins & Allen XL Double Action. This was one of a large number of budget priced revolvers marketed with names like Captain Jack, and Mountain Eagle. They were

five-shot, solid-frame weapons, produced in a variety of calibres. This gun is .32.

5 Manhattan Navy. The Manhattan Arms Company was one of many manufacturers who began to manufacture Colt-style revolvers once Colt's patent expired. The guns were well made and over 80,000 were produced. Colt took legal action to try to prevent their production.

6 Marlin XXX 1872 Revolver. John Marlin, a former employee of Colt, began revolver production when Rollin White's patent expired in 1869. Some 27,000 of this .30 caliber, center-fire revolver were produced between 1872 and 1877.

7 Metropolitan Navy. This gun was manufactured in 1864, when the Colt factory was damaged by fire. The Metropolitan models were almost indistinguishable from the Colt originals of the time.

8 Nepperhan Revolver. This was manufactured during the civil war as a copy of the .31 caliber Colt. Over 5,000 were made.

9 Remington Model 1861 Army. This was a solid, reliable, and popular weapon. Many thousands were made during the Civil War. Afterwards, they were available for use on the Frontier.

10 Remington Model 1861 Navy. This gun was referred to as the "Old Model Navy." It followed the same design as the Army version but in .36 caliber. Thousands also saw wartime service.

11 Remington Army Model 1875. This was Remington's answer to the Colt Model 1873. It was a single-action gun, produced in .44 and .45 calibers. The weapon never really challenged the Colt, but Remington always had its supporters.

12 Remington New Model Police Revolver. This was Remington's response to the plethora of Colt Police and Pocket

revolvers. It had a single-action arm in .36 caliber, and a 3-inch barrel. It was a compact, concealable weapon that could pack a hefty punch.

13 Remington Conversion Revolver. This gun is an example of one of the many revolvers that were converted to fire cartridge ammunition when the Rollin White patent expired in 1869. This is a New Model Pocket Revolver in .38 caliber.

14 Smith & Wesson Model 2 Army Revolver. This was available at the beginning of the Civil War and was an immediate success as it fired rimfire cartridges. Over 77,000 examples were sold between 1861 and 1874.

15 Smith & Wesson Model 3 Schofield. This gun was developed by Major George Schofield, as a heavy cavalry revolver. It was ordered by the Government in 1875. However, due to the pre-eminence of the Colt Single Action, stocks were sold off in 1887. The majority found their way to the

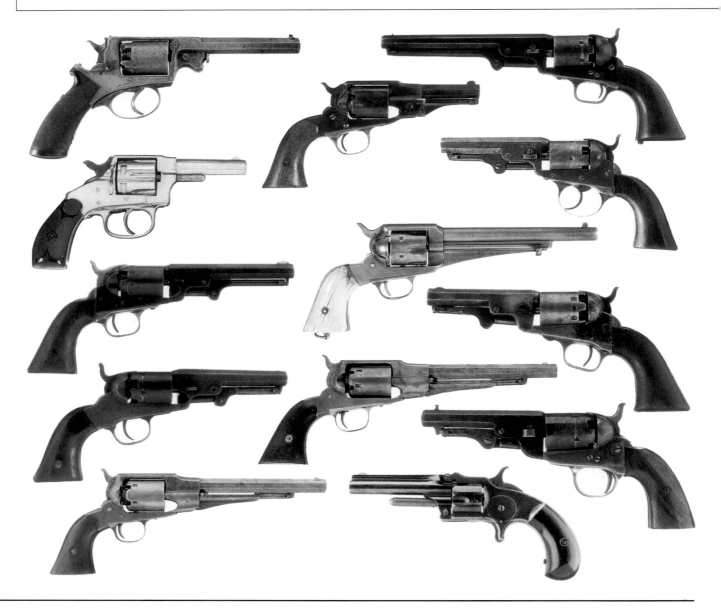

Western Frontier, and many fell into the hands of outlaws, such as Frank and Jesse James, and Bill Tilghman.

16 Smith & Wesson Model 3 Russian. The gun got its name from a large order that Colt received from the Russian Army for a gun that could use a special .44 caliber Russian "necked" cartridge. These guns also made their way into the domestic market.

17 Spiller & Burr Revolver. This was one of the products of the CSA armory in Macon, Georgia, during the Civil War. It was based on the Whitney 1858 Navy Revolver but due to the chronic lack of materials in the South, it was made from brass and iron, rather than steel. This example appears to have has made its way West, with the addition of brass studs on the handgrips. These were a hallmark of Indian ownership.

18 Starr Army Revolver Model 1863. Over 32,000 of this single-action revolver were produced between 1863 and 1865. The gun had an 8-inch barrel and fired a .44 rimfire cartridge.

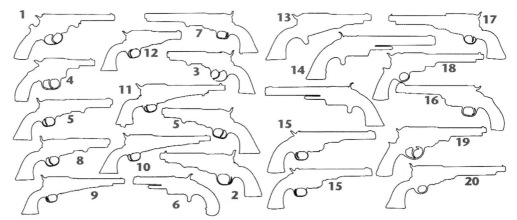

19 Starr Model 1858 Navy Revolver. This is a double-action revolver in .36 caliber. It has a 6-inch barrel.

20 Whitney Navy Revolver. Over 33,000 of this popular revolver were made. Unlike the Colt, the Whitney had a solid frame with an integral top strap above the cylinder. This made it stronger and more robust in service. Many survived to see action on the Frontier.

WINCHESTER RIFLES

1 Henry Rifle. Henry Rifle. This rifle was invented and patented by B.Tyler Henry and is chambered for a .44 cartridge, carried in a 15-round tubular magazine. At the time, its firepower gave it a natural advantage, but reloading was cumbersome. Also, the barrel grew hot after repeated fire causing the firer's left hand to burn, while slots in the tubular magazine allowed dirt to enter.

2 Winchester Model 1866 Sporting Rifle. This was produced by the newly formed Winchester Repeating Arms Company, formerly the Henry Repeating Rifle Company. The problems of the earlier Henry were solved in this model. It has a 24.4-inch barrel, a wooden forend grip, and a sealed 17-round magazine, loaded through a slot in the right-side plate.

3 Winchester 1866 Carbine. This gun was known as the "Yellow Boy" because of the distinctive color of its brass side plates. The reduced barrel length of 20 inches meant that the tubular magazine was shorter, holding only 13 rounds. John Wayne made the model famous in the movie *True Grit*, where the gun is modified with a loop-under lever, which enables him to reload and fire one handed, while riding.

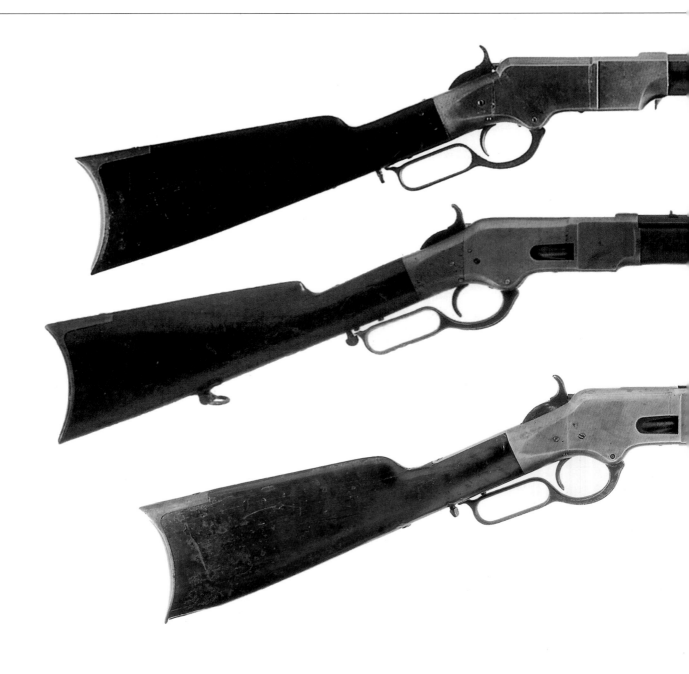

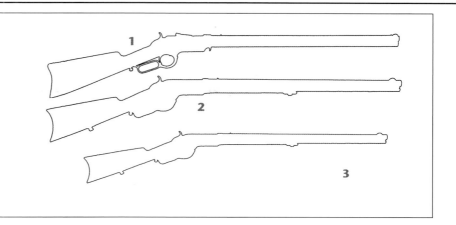

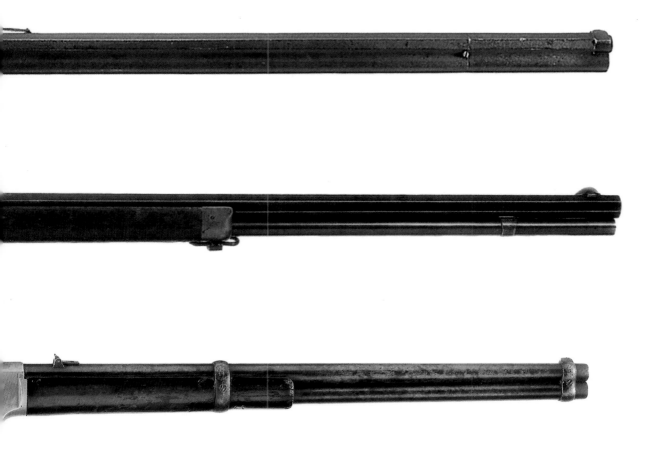

WINCHESTER MODEL 1873

Winchester Model 1873. The Model 1873 was an improvement on the earlier variant in three important respects. First, it had a stronger steel frame. Second, a dustcover was fitted over the action. Third, the gun was chambered to share ammunition with the Colt Single Action Revolver. This meant that the two guns were a synergetic choice when deciding which combination of sidearm and rifle to buy. 720,000 Model 1873s had been sold when production ended in 1919.

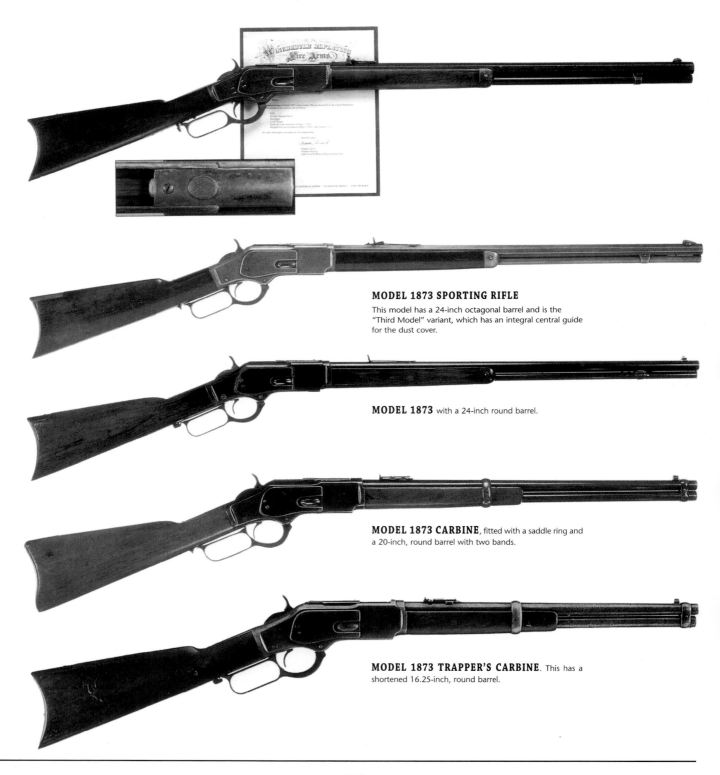

MODEL 1873 SPORTING RIFLE
This model has a 24-inch octagonal barrel and is the "Third Model" variant, which has an integral central guide for the dust cover.

MODEL 1873 with a 24-inch round barrel.

MODEL 1873 CARBINE, fitted with a saddle ring and a 20-inch, round barrel with two bands.

MODEL 1873 TRAPPER'S CARBINE. This has a shortened 16.25-inch, round barrel.

Model 1876

The Model 1876 incorporated changes necessitated by the more powerful cartridges that were coming into use. It had a larger more robust receiver. The sporting rifle version shown here had a 28-inch, round barrel together with a correspondingly longer forend.

Model 1886

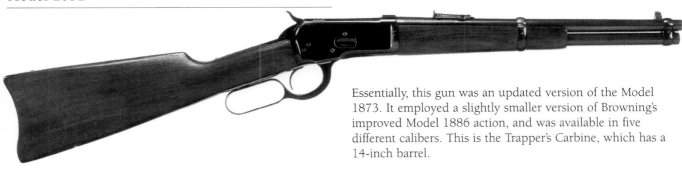

The Model 1886 was designed by John Moses Browning. It was designed to handle the more powerful center-fire cartridges that were becoming available. There were three basic configurations of the weapon: rifle, musket, and carbine. The rifle option was available in five different variants, including the sporting, "fancy" sporting, and takedown models. This version is the lightweight model, fitted with a shortened magazine and a cut back forend.

Model 1892

Essentially, this gun was an updated version of the Model 1873. It employed a slightly smaller version of Browning's improved Model 1886 action, and was available in five different calibers. This is the Trapper's Carbine, which has a 14-inch barrel.

Model 1894

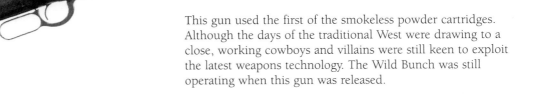

This gun used the first of the smokeless powder cartridges. Although the days of the traditional West were drawing to a close, working cowboys and villains were still keen to exploit the latest weapons technology. The Wild Bunch was still operating when this gun was released.

Model 1885

The Winchester Model 1885 used the first patent that the company bought from John M. Browning. It was the first single-shot rifle to be manufactured by the company. Winchester manufactured 139,000 of these weapons between 1885 and 1920. There were two variants: the "High Wall" and "Low Wall." The difference was defined by the angle of the frame where it covers the hammer. On the Low Wall version, the frame leaves the hammer and breech visible. On the High Wall version, only the spur of the hammer is visible.

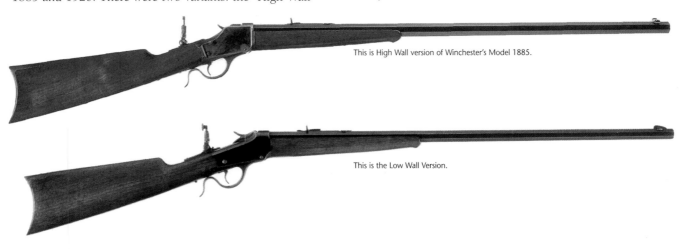

This is High Wall version of Winchester's Model 1885.

This is the Low Wall Version.

Model 1890

This Winchester model was also designed by the Browning Brothers. It was the company's first-ever slide-action rifle. It achieved great popularity, selling over 775,000 units. The gun was a late entry in the story of the West, but was a great little hunting gun for the trail.

Model 1895

John Browning's Model 1895 was the first Winchester lever-action rifle to feature a box magazine. In this case, it was non-detachable, and held five rounds. The gun received the highest possible endorsement when it was adopted by Theodore Roosevelt as his favorite hunting rifle.

SHARPS RIFLES

Christian Sharps set up his own firearms company in 1851, based in Hartford, Connecticut. He developed a range of single-shot, breech-loading rifles that became very popular during the Civil War. In the post-War years, the gun found favor with sportsmen and hunters, particularly in the West.

Sharps 1852 Saddle ring Carbine

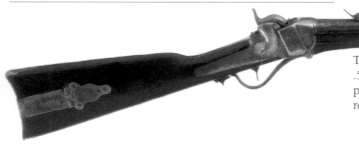

This gun is one of Christian Sharps's earlier designs: a neat .52 caliber single-shot cavalry carbine that used the Sharps patent pellet primer, mounted on the lock plate. This is recognizable by the slanting breech on the side of the frame.

Sharps New Model Carbine

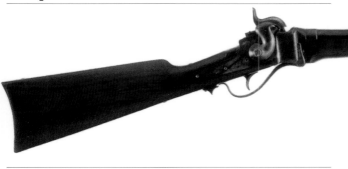

This weapon featured the "Straight Breech," with the Sharps pellet priming system integrated into the lockplate. The gun was an improved version of the Model 1852.

Sharps Sharpshooter Rifle

This gun was based on the Sharps New Model 1859 breech-loading rifle. It was modified with an extra hair trigger. The weapon was issued to Berdan's Sharpshooters in the Civil War. It also made an excellent long-range weapon on the Frontier.

Sharps Model 1874 Sporting Rifle Buffalo Gun

This gun was a direct competitor to the Winchester 1873. It is chambered for 45-70 ammunition and has a 28-inch barrel stamped "Old Reliable." This is how Sharps rifles were perceived. The gun was also available in .50 caliber and with a 30-inch barrel. The weapon was largely responsible for wiping out the herds of Plains buffalo.

SPENCER

Christopher M. Spencer was born in 1841. Initially, he made his weapons at South Manchester, Connecticut, but moved to Boston in 1862. Spencer's range of repeating rifles (equipped with 7-shot magazines) made a real difference to Union forces during the Civil War. Immediately after that conflict, the U.S. Army used Spencers in the Indian Wars. Foolishly, a revised gun was issued to the troops, fitted with a device known as the Stabler cutoff. This converted the Spencer to a single shot weapon. It was erroneously believed that soldiers would aim more carefully if they only had one shot. It is also likely that the revised version was designed to save money, as it was felt that repeating weapons squandered ammunition. Spencer went out of business in 1869 as the profits of the successful war years dwindled.

Model 1860 Spencer Repeating Carbine

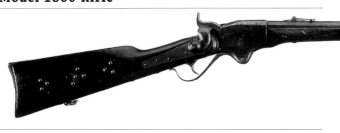

Personally endorsed by President Lincoln after he witnessed a field trial, this gun was one of the most charismatic weapons of the Civil War. After the War, it was widely available for civilian use. The gun fired a .52 caliber rimfire straight copper cartridge.

Model 1860 Rifle

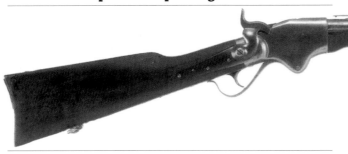

This rifle was similar to the carbine, but had a longer, 30-inch barrel, which was fully stocked, almost to the muzzle. The stock was fitted with an iron forend cap, and three barrel-bands.

Model 1865 Carbine

This later model of the Spencer carbine had a shorter 20-inch barrel, and was chambered for .50 cartridge, which had been adapted for use in the Indian Wars. The lighter but more powerful 56-50 cartridge improved the gun's ballistic performance. In a close fight, like that at Beecher's Island, repeating rifles were hard to beat. They were also prized by Westerners as a handy saddle gun.

Spencer Sporting Rifle

After the Civil War, Spencer produced weapons for the civilian market. This hunting rifle is chambered for .45 caliber ammunition, and has a 32-inch barrel. Many of these guns were adapted for Western use by gunsmiths in Denver and San Francisco. This one has been altered by A.J. Plate of San Francisco.

SPRINGFIELD

Springfield, Massachusetts was one of the National Armory sites founded by George Washington in 1777. The area continued to play an important part in the development of military firearms, in the years leading up to, and during, the Civil War. Springfield's Master Armorer, Erskine S. Allin, invented the "Trapdoor" method of converting rifles to breech-loaders.

Springfield Spencer Conversion Rifle

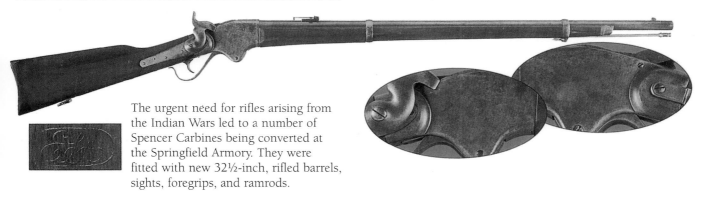

The urgent need for rifles arising from the Indian Wars led to a number of Spencer Carbines being converted at the Springfield Armory. They were fitted with new 32½-inch, rifled barrels, sights, foregrips, and ramrods.

Springfield Indian Carbine

This Indian-made weapon was converted by hand from a Springfield Musket. It features a cut-down barrel (21¾ inches from the original 44), a shortened forend. Its barrel band is made from cloth and sinew. The stock is decorated with the characteristic brass tacks.

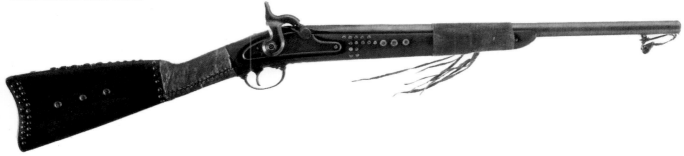

Springfield Models 1873 and 1879

This Indian-made weapon was converted by hand from a Springfield Musket. It features a cut-down barrel (21¾ inches from the original 44), a shortened forend. Its barrel band is made from cloth and sinew. The stock is decorated with the characteristic brass tacks.

WESTERN SHOTGUNS

The shotgun is ideal for close-range defense and offense, and was used by lawmen and outlaws alike. Shotguns are usually loaded with lead pellets or buckshot, and are fired from the hip. This results in terrible devastation at short range, without the need for taking careful aim. They were used by Wells Fargo guards, sheriffs, and bank robbers as well as homesteaders and ranchers.

Parker Shotgun

Charles Parker's sons took over his company in 1868. They recognized the peacetime need for shotguns, and designed this classic side-by-side shotgun with external hammers. Many owners had the barrels of their Parker shotgun shortened.

Remington Model 1889 Wells Fargo

This Model 1889 was part of a special order for Wells Fargo. It has had its barrels shortened to make it easier for stagecoach drivers to draw the weapon. They used the gun to defend themselves from robbery and attack.

Roper Revolving Shotgun

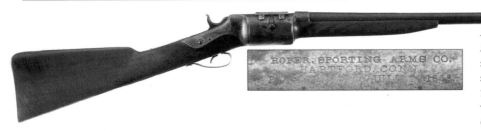

After the Civil War, the Roper Sporting Arms Company designed a revolving shotgun. It was equipped with four steel cartridges, which could be reloaded with shot and powder. These were fitted into a cylindrical housing. Colt produced a similar revolving shotgun, based on the design of their revolving rifle.

Winchester Model 1887 Lever Action Shotgun

This Browning-designed gun was sold with either a 30- or 32-inch barrel, in either 10- or 12-gauge. The five-shot magazine was housed in a tube under the barrel. A Riot version was also available, with a 20-inch barrel. The Model was a favorite with the Texas Rangers.

OTHER WESTERN RIFLES

As the century wore on, new technology overtook some of the earlier of weapons that dated from the Civil War. All guns were now breech-loading, and ammunition was more sophisticated and powerful. Specialist gunsmiths adapted guns to customer's preferences, and a huge range of sporting, target, and hunting rifles was offered to a growing market.

Remington No1 Sporting Rifle

This gun employed Remington's famous Rolling Block action. It has a 28-inch barrel chambered for .44 caliber center fire cartridges.

Colt Revolving Carbine

This gun was patented on September 10th 1855, and was available in various calibers, including .36, .44, and .56. It also came in various barrel lengths, ranging from 15 to 24 inches. The rifle version was issued to Berdan's Sharpshooters at the beginning of the Civil War. But the Sharpshooters abandoned the gun in favor of the Sharps rifle. The large caliber cylinder held five shots, while the .44 and .36 versions held six shots.

Marlin Model 1881

This was Marlin's first lever-action rifle. 20,000 were sold on the Western Frontier This example is made in .40-60 caliber, and has a 24-inch octagonal barrel. Marlin remains a name in the lever action market to this day.

George C.Schoyen's Winchester High Wall Rifle

Schoyen built up a very successful custom-made rifle business, based in Denver. He favored single-shot guns, and specialized in "Schutzen" styles.

DERINGERS AND VEST GUNS

As the West progressed, a new breed of men arrived. Clad in tailored jackets and dust-free Derby hats, the gamblers had hit town. Unlike the cowboys, these men did not wear large Colts holstered in plain view, preferring to hide small but deadly, short-barreled guns about their person. These were often concealed in a vest pocket, inside a hatband, or in a well-tailored sleeve. Guns like these settled many an accusation of cheating. Guns like these were also popular with saloon girls, and more respectable ladies. They were ideal for self-defense, and could be concealed in a purse or a garter. Here is a selection of these weapons of concealment.

1 Tipping & Lawden 4-barrel pistol
Four barrels are better than one. Master Gunsmiths Tipping & Lawden of Birmingham, England manufactured this Sharps design. It was then imported into The United States. The gun has 3-inch barrels and is .31 caliber. It is lavishly decorated with much engraving, and pearl grips.

2 ,3, 4 Colt Deringers
These are three examples of the Colt Third Model Deringer. The gun was designed by Alexander Thuer, and was often known as the "Thuer Derringer." All three examples are .41 caliber weapons with 2½-inch barrels. The barrels pivoted to one side for loading.

5 Hammond Bulldog
This is a crudely finished single-shot self-defense weapon of .44 caliber. Nevertheless, it would be effective at close range. It has a 4-inch barrel and must have kicked like a mule!

6 Hopkins & Allen Vest Pocket Deringer
This cleverly camouflaged trinket was just 1¾ inches long, and fired a .22 caliber round. It

could (literally) fit in the palm of the shooter's hand, and concealed until the last moment.

7 National No2 Deringer
Moore's Patent Firearm Company was established in Brooklyn in the mid-nineteenth century. The company changed its name to The National Arms Company in 1866. This gun is the No. 2 Model. It has a spur trigger, and is loaded by dropping the barrel down to one side. Following the takeover of the company by Colt in 1870, this design was marketed as the Colt No. 2 Deringer.

8 Remington Elliot Ring Trigger Pistol
This pistol relied on four solid static barrels to deliver four shots. It was chambered for .32 caliber ammunition. The ring trigger was pushed forward to rotate the firing pin, then pulled back to cock the mechanism and fire.

9 Remington No2 Vest Pocket Pistol
Designed by Joseph Rider, this .32 caliber vest pocket pistol fired a single shot. It was equipped with the unique Rider split-breech

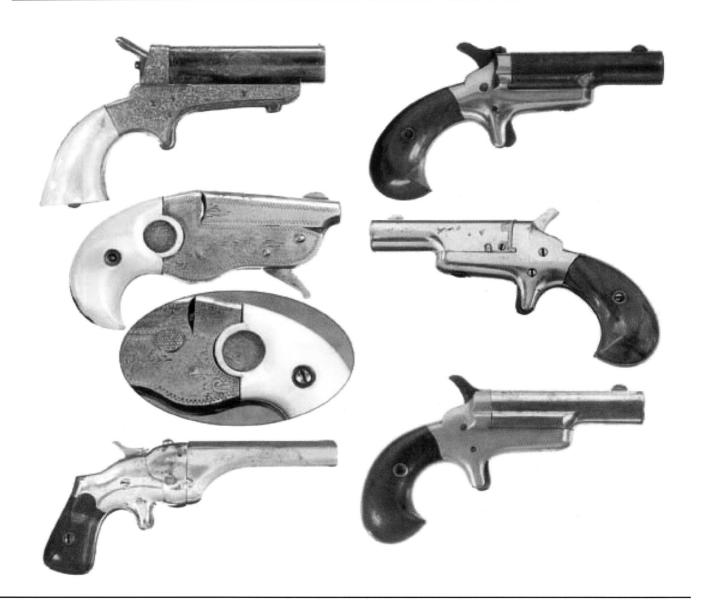

loading system, and had a 3¼-inch barrel.

10 Remington Double Deringer
This was the ultimate design for last ditch defense. The over-and-under barrel layout was less cumbersome and heavy than that of multi-barrel guns. The gun was also reliable, and fired two rounds in .41 caliber: an assailant-stopping load. The gun became extremely popular and over 150,000 were manufactured between 1866 and 1935.

11 Sharps pepperbox
Strictly speaking, this design by master gunsmith Christian Sharps is a multi-barreled pistol rather than a pepperbox. Nonetheless, the gun became a very popular weapon. The gun was reloaded by sliding the barrel block forward along a rail to access the breech. The four-barrel system was static and the firing pin rotated to fire each chamber in turn.

12 Wheeler Double Deringer
This weapon was designed and manufactured by the American Arms Company. It features two vertically-mounted barrels that were

rotated manually. This example has a 3-inch barrel block, chambered for two .32 caliber rounds. It has a nickel-plated frame, a spur trigger, and blued barrels.

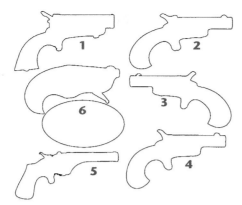
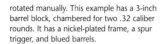
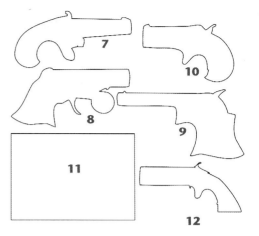

WESTERN CHARACTERS

Perhaps nowhere in the history of the world has a region spawned so many familiar and fascinating characters as the Old West. A flood of individualists, mavericks, eccentrics, and loners filled the Western stage for over a century, and has passed into American folklore.

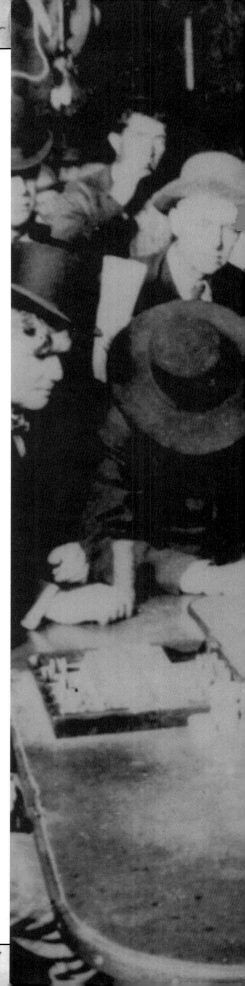

Right: Faro was a popular Western game of chance.

MOUNTAIN MEN

The Mountain Men were some of the first and toughest characters to make the trek West. The very first of these rugged individualists journeyed to the frontier in 1822, as part of the Ashley-Henry expedition. William Ashley advertised for a hundred "enterprising young men," whose goal was to break the Hudson Bay Company's stranglehold on the area's fur trade in favor of his Rocky Mountain Fur Company. Setting the tone of things to come, one member of the group, Jedediah Strong Smith had an ear ripped off in a grizzly bear attack. His companions sewed the ear back on as best they could, but he was known for wearing his hair long after this unfortunate incident.

The mountain men soon developed a thriving trapping industry exploiting the natural resources of the Rockies. In a system devised by William Ashley, they traded their pelts at annual "rendezvous." These meetings were times of great festivity, after the extreme ardors of the hunting season. Mountain man James Beckwourth described the celebrations as consisting of "mirth, song, dancing, shouting, trading,

Above: Jim Beckworth was one of the most notable mountain men. He was half African American.

Left: A painting by Joe Grandee depicting the archetypal mountain man with fringed jacket, plains rifle, powder horn, and skinning knife.

running, jumping, singing, racing, target-shooting, yarns, frolic, with all sorts of extravaganzas that white men or Indians could invent." Vast quantities of whiskey were also consumed. An easterner described the mountain men "as crazy a set of men as I ever saw."

Characters like Jim Bridger and Kit Carson epitomized the positive image of the mountain man. Bridger was fortunate to have a constitution of iron that enabled him to survive massive hardship, and he was a famous storyteller. Carson was renowned for his feats of bravery and marksmanship. Like Bridger (and many other trappers), he married an Indian wife, Singing Grass. Both men embodied the good-hearted toughness that typified these extraordinary characters.

Bridger and Carson were actually one of a relatively select club. Even during the heyday of the fur trade, in the decade between 1820 and 1830, only around a thousand mountain men roamed the West. Contrary to the popular image of the lonesome trapper, deprived of human company for months at

Above: A rendez vous of mountain men took place every year during the 1820s.

Below: Kit Carson and his fellow trappers gather round a roaring campfire to yarn away the evening.

Above: Trappers and hunters led a very Spartan way of life, sheltering in deserted cabins whenever they could.

a time, only a few men hunted alone. It was much more common for bands of trappers to trek through the mountains together, sharing a traveling camp.

Although the fur trade was largely finished by 1840, the brief heyday of the mountain men quickly passed into legend. This was because their lives were genuinely extraordinary. As Francis Parkman wrote in his 1849 The Oregon Trail, "I defy the annals of chivalry to furnish the record of a life more wild and perilous that that of a Rocky Mountain trapper." Not only did they have to brave extreme environmental perils of heat exhaustion and exposure, but they also had to contend with starvation, dehydration, and attack from both Indians and animals. Their lives were governed by the seasons, and to succeed, the mountain men had to be completely in tune with nature. It is ironic that this organic lifestyle led to the virtual extermination of the fur-bearing animals of the frontier.

FRONTIER PREACHERS

One of the many inspirations that brought men to the West was religion. Some were looking for a new Zion, while others came into the region as missionaries, to bring the word of God to the heathen settlers of the frontier.

Organized religion was certainly not one of the first priorities for most Western towns. Saloons were usually built long before churches were, and in far greater numbers. The town mostly had a decidedly secular atmosphere. Hard-working miners and cowhands were far more likely to spend their single day of rest in the saloon than in piety. Even if they had wanted them, Bibles were scare on the frontier, and difficult to obtain. Several town newspapers tried to influence their readers into living more civilized lives, which would include some religious observance, particularly on Sundays. Several preacher-editors, whose specific aim was to reduce godlessness in the West, established frontier newspapers, and

Above: Lorenzo Dow was such a powerful outdoor preacher that many children were named after him.

Above: Worship often took place in hastily converted barns.

Above: An old print showing an outdoor religious gathering in the West.

Right: A traveling preacher's saddlebags.

Above: *Harper's Weekly* depicts the plight of a travelling preacher.

Above: The Revered Samson Occum was a Native American Presbyterian preacher.

tried to preach to their readers while bringing the news. Few had much success.

But as the region became more widely settled, many Westerners came to believe that a church would ensure the survival of their town, and confirm that their community had moved on from its rough and ready beginnings. But organized religion found it difficult to function in the raw Western settlements, where a culture of free-living had taken a deep hold. Most had made the journey West for material reasons, and were too preoccupied with survival and making money to worry about their spiritual lives. Drinking was epidemic, and Eastern-style Temperance Societies unknown.

With no churches to shelter them; most frontier preachers were forced to accept a traveling vocation. They usually relied on their own personal interpretations of faith, unaffiliated to any particular denomination. They rode extensive circuits, preaching and converting as they went, reclaiming the "lost

souls" of the West. Many visited settlers in their own rough cabins, and shared their simple victuals and accommodation. They also shared their hardships, and often went without food all together. A circuit preacher could only expect to make around $30 to $50 a year.

Evangelical Methodists comprised the first organized church to have an impact on the West. Methodist preachers sparked the so-called "Great Revival" in early frontier religion. The Baptists and the Cumberland Presbyterians also became popular sects out West. More introspective religious groups like the Episcopalians found it extremely difficult to establish themselves on the frontier. They were slow to recruit new members, and found it almost impossible to survive outside of the towns.

Organized religion quickly changed Western life. Perhaps its most important contribution was the way it brought groups of settlers together, helping to establish a more cohesive society. These sincere Christians also tried to foster the settlers' finer qualities, and discouraged the morally lax atmosphere of the region. Their informal religious gatherings were used as an excuse for neighbors to get together and enjoy each other's hospitality, and were far removed from the formal church services of the East.

Frontier preachers often came from similar backgrounds to the settlers they served, and most were not well educated. Some had only ever read the Bible, but found this sufficient for their needs. Their meager stipends meant that most preachers had to work in other jobs to support their families, and this kept them in close touch with the hardships of their "flock." Their lack of formal education meant that their preaching style was often intensely personal, and direct. They spoke the unadorned truth, which greatly appealed to the simple frontiers folk.

Many preachers had also shared the same terrible sufferings as their brethren. The famous Tennessee preacher Reuben Ross worked as a farmer for five days a week. He had had a dreadful start in the frontier, losing five of his children in his first five years out West. Despite this, his sermons were full of encouragement and comfort. Another preacher with only limited education, but a brilliant gift for self-expression, was John Taylor. A Kentucky Baptist firebrand, Taylor published the famous *A History of Ten Baptist Churches* in 1823, which paints a very accurate picture of religion on the frontier. He was notorious for his extremely passionate sermons, said to make women weep and strong men tremble.

Some preachers didn't even wait until they reached the West to start their work. Martin Peterson took an emigrant train to Oregon in 1864, and had made thirty onboard converts before he reached his destination. He held a daily service as the train rumbled west.

The early frontier had very few church buildings, and many preachers addressed their flock outdoors. These first Western sermons were delivered in idyllic settings that must have reminded these godly men of the Garden of Eden. Reuben Ross often delivered his sermons from under a spreading oak tree, while his audience sat on the ground around his feet. The warmth and simplicity of these camp-meeting gatherings attracted many settlers, who enjoyed the cheerful songs and easily understood sermons. In her poem *Before the Wedding*, Marion Davies described how the preacher "told the Gospel story, so thrillingly, through all the grove." Religion in the West was fresh and new, free from the stifling conventions of the East.

These camp-meeting services also challenged the surprisingly hierarchical nature of frontier society. Men were divided from women, whites from blacks, and rich from poor. This straightforward form of religion drew them all together, as the Reverend W. I. Ellsworth described, "What a scene to gaze upon! There was bowed the sire and the son, the man of wealth and the man of penury, the dweller in the city and the dweller in the country, side by side, seeking the same Savior." The Revered Gustavus Hines particularly commended the easily understood rhetoric of frontier sermons, where there was "no mincing the truth of God's word." The meetings also provided a welcome diversion from the drinking and brawling of most Western gatherings.

While plainness and clarity were often the keys to a preacher's success, hard work was also effective. Prolific preacher Peter Cartwright converted over 10,000 souls in the course of his extremely active ministry. He often held meetings by both day and by night to bring as many westerners to Christ as possible.

The itinerant preachers of the rugged West often had to

Above: Peter Cartwright converted over 10,000 souls.

overcome far worse than inclement weather, and rowdy hecklers. They had to use all their grit and resolve to follow their vocation. Western preachers often required actual physical courage. Horseback minister Oscar Elmer was bold enough to stroll into the saloons of Fargo and invite the patrons to his evangelical meetings. He explained that he "made it a study to…win these men from their profanity. Many of them are kind hearted but being away from the influence of house and society is very rough." Other preachers took camp-meeting discipline rather far in dealing with their rough and ready flock. Tennessee preacher John Brooks once threw a blasphemous man into a large fire and claimed to have held him there with his foot until he repented. Circuit preachers were often obliged to carry a weapon for self-defense, and many pistol-packing men of God became notorious for their fights with outlaws, Indians, and wild animals.

The weather itself could also confound the preacher's best efforts. Unable to reach his audience across a storm-swollen river, Preacher Garner McConnio preached from the opposite bank, raising his voice over the rushing torrent.

But not all of the horseback preachers were completely pure in heart. Some used dubious methods to achieve conversions. Some employed violent coercion, while the highly charged atmosphere of some meetings developed sexual overtones. Prostitutes patrolled the edges of these corrupted ministries, hunting for clients.

There was already something of a backlash against the traveling preachers from other frontiersmen, and the bad behavior of a few focused the descent. Many Western men were perfectly happy with their independent lives, unfettered by religion and social conventions. These men considered preachers interfering, and unmanly. Writers such as Mark Twain and Hardin E. Taliaferro fanned these flames of contempt by satirizing the worst of the preachers as licentious predators, corrupt and greedy hypocrites.

In modern times, the preacher character in Western novels and movies is often highly ambiguous. In Clint Eastwood's 1985 film, *Pale Rider*, The preacher is an avenging figure on the side of good, but is violent and remorseless. Eli Sunday, preacher in the 2007 movie *There Will be Blood* is entirely good, but weak, and no match for the wicked Daniel Plainview. The minister in the iconic *High Noon* is notionally decent, but is too feeble to stand on the side of justice with Gary Cooper's marshal character. By contrast, the gunslinger-turned-preacher in the Frank Sinatra film, *Johnny Concho*

(1956) actively protects the worthless Concho from avenging bandits. Con men disguised as preachers are also stock Western characters. Harry Bellafonte puts an unusual spin on this cliché in the 1972 all-black Western, *Buck and the Preacher*.

PONY EXPRESS RIDERS

Despite being one of the shortest-lived institutions of the Old West, the Pony Express has achieved a legendary status. This is undoubtedly due to the extraordinary caliber of the mail riders themselves. These men (or boys, as most of them were) have become synonymous with extreme courage, resilience, and toughness. Their spirit was the essence of the West itself. Not only did they have to counter the rigors of the trail and the dramatic weather conditions of the region, but also attacks from Indians and wild animals.

William H. Russell established the Pony Express in 1859, and set up a company with his partners William B. Waddell and Alexander Majors. His ambition was to deliver mail from coast to coast in ten days or less, all year round, and cut the existing stagecoach delivery time in half. Russell's Central Overland California, and Pikes Peak Express Company carefully worked out a 1,966-mile trail between St. Joseph, Missouri, and Sacramento, California. It crossed plains, prairies, and deserts, and scaled mountain passes. To make the immense journey possible, Russell established stations at approximately ten-mile intervals; employed four hundred station hands, purchased five hundred horses, and arranged for Iowan grain to be shipped to each station. He also

Above: : A deserted Pony Express station.

Right: Clint Eastwood plays a travelling preacher in the movie *Pale Rider*.

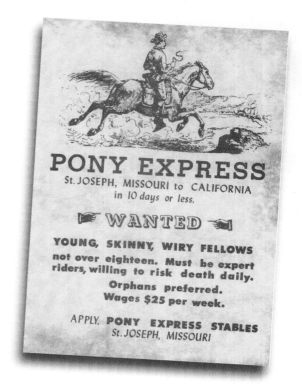

Left and above: Photograph of Pony Express rider, Frank E. Webner, and William H. Russell's recruitment poster for young riders.

advertised for express riders, specifying that he wanted "young, skinny, wiry fellows not over eighteen...expert riders, willing to risk death daily. Orphans preferred." He wasn't joking, but had soon gathered the two hundred candidates he needed. Most were younger than twenty years of age, and weighed less than 125 pounds. For their death-defying efforts, they were paid between $100 and $150 a month.

Before they could ride for the Pony Express, each rider had to take an oath of service, stating, "I agree not to use profane language, not to get drunk, not to gamble, not to treat animals cruelly and not to do anything else that is incompatible with the conduct of a gentleman." Each rider covered between 75 and 100 miles a day at the gallop, with an average speed of 10 miles per hour. They changed their mounts for fresh ones at the stations Russell had established.

The Pony Express mail service started on April 3, 1860. According to legend, John Fry was the first westbound rider, and James Randall the first to ride to the east.

Many notable Westerners rode for the Pony Express in their youth, including Wild Bill Hickok, Buffalo Bill Cody, and Calamity Jane. The service attracted, and needed, tough characters. Bronco Bill Charlie was the youngest ever Pony Express rider, signed up at the age of eleven. The riders soon became an important part of Western life, charting the course of history with the documents they carried. Robert "Pony Bob" Haslam, for example, made an epic ride to deliver the news of Lincoln's election. Despite being shot through the jaw and losing three teeth, Haslam continued on his way. The service also delivered a copy of Lincoln's March 1861 Inaugural Address to Congress in a record seven days and seven hours. Bill Cody himself made the longest non-stop ride in the history of the service, when he found his relief rider had been murdered at his post. He covered 322 miles non-stop, using 21 fresh horses. Cody's regular route was the forty-five mile stretch west of Julesburg, Colorado.

Each Pony Express rider was equipped with a specially

designed mailbag, or mochila, complete with four locked leather compartments, or cantinas. Each rider used the bag to carry a maximum of twenty pounds in weight, which included his personal equipment. This consisted of a water sac, a Bible (courtesy of Alexander Majors), a knife, a revolver, and a horn to alert the managers of the relay stages. To save weight, and ensure that the riders carried as much mail as possible, their equipment was ultimately pared down to just the water and revolver. Originally, Pony Express mail was charged at $5 per half ounce, but to make the service more attractive, this was reduced to $2.50, and finally to $1.

Despite the high repute of the Pony Express, the company was never financially sound. Its money problems were compounded when it failed to win a $1 million mail contract from Congress. But the final blow to the service was new technology: the telegraph. When the poles of the Creighton Telegraph Line reached Salt Lake City in October 1861, the mail service became obsolete overnight. It ceased operations

two days later. The directors lost over $200,000 in the enterprise, the equivalent of millions of dollars today. Despite their entrepreneurship, two of the original Pony Express directors died in poverty. Only the God-fearing Majors made a successful new career, working for the Union Pacific Railroad.

In its short period of operation, the Pony Express riders covered over 650,000 miles, and delivered 34,753 pieces of mail, with the loss of only one mailbag. A single rider had been lost, killed by an arrow shot by a Plains warrior. In 1866, the company's assets were sold to Wells Fargo Overland Mail Company for $1.5 million. Wells Fargo continued to use the Pony Express logo for its armored car service until 2001.

Despite its brief period of survival, the Pony Express had a huge impact on the West, and has become an integral part of its romance. Perhaps its greatest achievement was psychological. The service broke the isolation of the Western settlers, by bringing them news from the seat of government. Many believe that it helped to preserve the Union itself by drawing East and West closer together, helping to forge one nation.

Russell's route between St. Joseph and Sacramento proved to have been very skillfully worked out, and was followed by the Union Pacific Railroad. It is now shadowed by US 36, which is known as The Pony Express Highway.

GAMBLERS

"I assert, without fear of successful contradiction from those who know, that not one professional gambler in a thousand is at all times absolutely square."

From "Easy Money" by Harry Brolaski, 1911

Among the many types of men and women who came west to exploit other westerners, the gamblers were some of the most colorful. Gambling reflected the very character of the region, with its willingness to take chances, and its spirit of adventure. Almost every Western movie shows men, and

Above: A tin type photograph of four men enjoying a card game.

Right: A Currier and Ives print of a Mississippi River boat, these were a magnet to professional gamblers.

occasionally ladies, playing cards, roulette, or other games of chance. Gambling and liquor were the twin attractions of the thousands of saloons that spring up in the region, and became an integral part of frontier life.

As the rest of America became less tolerant of gambling and other forms of "vice" many professional gamblers made a strategic move west. Their first targets were the Mississippi riverboats, and it is estimated that between 600 and 800 "gamesmen" worked the boats in the 1840s. Famous gamblers like Charles Cora made huge fortunes on the river. Notorious as the Mississippi's foremost faro player, Cora was reputed to have won over $85,000 in six months. Riverboat gamblers Jimmy Fitzgerald and Charles Starr were equally renowned for their sartorial elegance. The originators of the riverboat gamblers' sharp dress code, the pair was always the epitome of good style. They sported expensive black suits and boots, ruffled white shirts, brocaded vests, conspicuous jewelry, and silver-topped walking canes.

Right: A Faro game at the Orient Saloon, Bisbee, Arizona, circa 1900.

But as the riverboats gave way to the railroads, the gamblers moved into the West itself to ply their trade.

The California Gold Rush had initiated a massive gambling boom on the West Coast, and San Francisco took over from New Orleans as America's gaming capital. The 1850s and 1860s were the Golden Age of gambling in California, and gold dust fortunes changed hands daily. The city's Portsmouth Square was the epicenter of the trade, and was ringed with gaming establishments. The Parker House was probably the most notorious of these, and it was said that over half a million dollars was won there nightly. The Parker House was flanked by two equally flamboyant enterprises, Samuel Dennison's Exchange and the El Dorado Gambling Saloon.

But violence and criminality also flourished in the wake of the gambling industry, and the citizens of San Francisco became increasingly intolerant, until the townsfolk lynched several card sharks. Feeling unwelcome, the gamblers followed the money to the region's mining and cow towns. Miners and cowhands rolled into saloons all over the West

with cash and gold dust burning holes in their jeans, and soon became prey.

Unsurprisingly, not all the games were on the level. A whole industry had sprung up to help professional card sharks fleece money from the gullible by manufacturing "gaffed" equipment, This included "advantaged cards," loaded dice, rigged roulette wheels, and faro layouts.

The Western gambling boom spawned any number of colorful characters, both male and female. Many professional gamblers were also gunmen, from both sides of the law, and were mighty quick on the draw.

Like many of his type, George Devol started out as a highly successful riverboat gambler, but moved to the frontier to further his career. He was also the author of a famous autobiography, Forty Years a Gambler on the Mississippi. In the course of his working life, Devol was involved in endless fights and skirmishes. He wrote that he had "been struck some terrible blows on my head with iron dray-pins, pokers, clubs, stone-coal, and bowlders (stet)." But he survived to win over $2 million in his playing career. Like so many gambling fortunes, Devol's money melted away like snow, and he died penniless. Easy come, easy go.

Wild Bill Hickok ended his wide-ranging career as a professional gambler. Always irascible, he shot Dave Tuff to death when the latter won his watch at cards. In fact, Hickok was generally drunk to be a successful player, and often took his winnings by violence rather than skill. In his final years, Hickok hurtled down a terrible spiral of drink, depravity, and

Above: N. C. Wyeth's painting of Will Bill Hickok unmasking a cheat at cards.

violence. Ultimately, he was shot to death while playing cards in Deadwood. His assassin was his fellow card shark, Jack McCall. As he died, Hickok held the now legendary "Dead Man's Hand:" the ace of spades, the ace of clubs, the eight of clubs, the eight of spades, and the queen or jack of diamonds.

One of the few Western gamblers to die in his bed, Dick Clark was also one of the most successful. He plied his trade in the traditional gambling towns of Tombstone and Deadwood, and became the owner of the Alhambra Saloon and Gambling Hall. Card playing partner of Wyatt Earp,

Clark became known as the "King of Gamblers," and inspired a generation of younger men. He died of tuberculosis in 1893.

Luke Short was one of Dick Clark's protégés. Short worked for Wyatt Earp in Tombstone's famous Oriental Saloon. He opened his own establishment, the famous Elephant Saloon in Fort Worth, Texas, which became a haunt of the most famous Western cardsharps. The Elephant hosted some of the era's most famous card games, whose players included Bat Masterson, Wyatt Earp, and Charlie Coe.

Soapy Smith was one of the gambling brotherhood's less reputable characters. Known as the "King of the frontier Con Men," he was known for his motto, "Get it while the gettin's good." Like many of his type, Soapy was also an

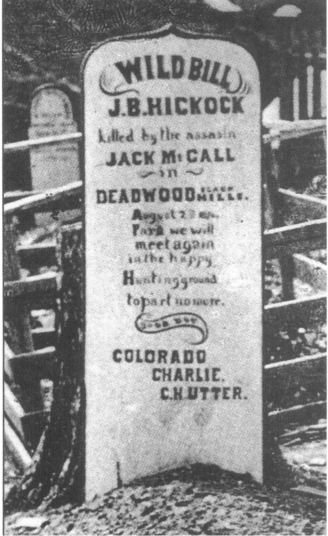

argumentative drunk who provoked the wrong man once too often. Fatally shot by the equally unpleasant Frank Reid, his last words are said to have been, "My god, don't shoot."

Thrown onto their own resources, several well-known Western women also took to the gaming tables, and their success often surpassed that of their male counterparts.

Lottie Deano inherited her love of gambling from her father. When her family sent her, unaccompanied, to Denver to find a suitable husband, she ran off with a highly unsuitable jockey, Johnny Golden. Golden proved his low caliber by introducing his young wife to riverboat gambling. But Lottie soon demonstrated her extraordinary ability. When

Above: Wild Bill Hickock's grave. Hickok was shot in 1876 during a card game in Deadwood, holding the famous "Dead Man's Hand."

Right: Luke Short was the proprietor of the famous Elephant Saloon in Fort Worth, Texas, which became the haunt of the most famous Western cardsharps.

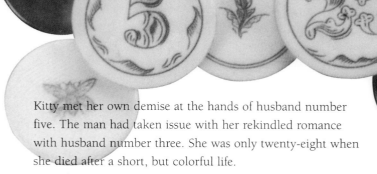

the couple split, she became the house gambler at San Antonio's University Club, and earned her moniker, the "Queen of the Pasteboards." Ultimately, Lottie married a wealthy banker, and became a society woman. She is immortalized as Gunsmoke's Miss Kitty.

Big Nose Kate, Doc Holliday's common law wife, made the career change from prostitution to card shark at his insistence. Having met in Bessie Earp's "sporting house," the pair traveled the West as professional card sharks, specializing in blackjack.

A rather better-looking woman, Poker Alice, used her feminine charms to mesmerize her fellow players. Born Alice Ivers, Poker Alice also came into the gambling trade through the influence of her husband. As a mining engineer, Frank often visited the camp "parlors" in company with his wife. Fascinated by the card play, Alice joined in, and proved herself extremely able. When Frank was killed in a mining accident, Alice supported herself by playing poker, and earned her famous nickname. She worked in gambling halls across Colorado, Oklahoma, and New Mexico, and earned a fortune, of up to $6,000 a night. Ultimately, Alice opened a brothel, and was particularly famous for her trademark cigar.

Kitty LeRoy was another famous female gambler, who was equally notorious as a bad-tempered shootist. Five times married; Kitty was the proprietor of Deadwood's Mint Gambling Saloon. Having shot at least one husband to death,

Kitty met her own demise at the hands of husband number five. The man had taken issue with her rekindled romance with husband number three. She was only twenty-eight when she died after a short, but colorful life.

As the West became more civilized, its citizens became tired of the explosive cocktail of gambling, drink, and vice that had resulted in so much violence, death, and disorder. Its townsfolk longed for the well-regulated and peaceful life typical of the East. Abilene, Texas longed for calm, but found it particularly difficult to control its gambling fraternity. Its marshal was none other than the famous drunk "short-card artist," Bill Hickok. As Bat Masterson wrote, "gambling was not only the principle and best-paying industry of the town at the time, but it was also reckoned among its most respectable."

Despite this, the State of California had outlawed gambling by the 1890s, and it was gradually driven into smaller and smaller enclaves across the West. The days of the professional gambler were gradually numbered, and few were nostalgic for the old days. Despite this, some Westerners were aware that the gradual control of gambling was symbolic of the loss of the untrammeled freedom of the frontier. It was a sign that the region was being gradually tamed, and becoming just like everywhere else.

GOLD DIGGERS

Perhaps gold diggers were the most frequently disillusioned Westerners. When James Marshall found gold nuggets glittering at the bottom of a ditch at Sutter's Mill, near Coloma in the Sierra Nevada, he must have thought that he had made his fortune. As he said, "it made my heart thump." In fact, Marshall didn't make a cent out of the extraordinary phenomenon he had started, and his employer, John Sutter, was ruined. Marshal found the nuggets in 1848. Later that year, President James Polk confirmed

Right: William Barclay Masterson, one of the Dodge City Gang appears in the guise of a sober citizen.

and many perished en route. They mostly came overland across the Oregon and California trails, and by sea through the Panama Shortcut and around Cape Horn. Even so, hundreds of thousands made it. As Louis L'Amour explained, they included "some good minin' men...outnumbered by the rowdies, the gamblers, the killers, the sneak thieves, short-card artists, and cutthroats." This was substantially true. Although the largest proportion of the miners were American, men also came from every corner of the world, including France, Germany, Turkey, Hawaii, China, Peru, New Zealand, Mexico, and Chile. 90,000 Chinese came to the region, making them the largest group. Most of these hopeful miners left their wives and families to weep for them back home, and many never saw them again.

These immigrants also included many desperate men; convicts from Australia, escaped slaves, and displaced Indians. Without any effective control, the region soon began to disintegrate into lawlessness. Merchant ships bringing goods into San Francisco became stranded as their crews deserted to try their luck in the goldfields, and the harbor became a sea of masts.

The first gold was easily collected by backbreaking

the discovery of Californian gold in Congress, and expressed his view that the discovery could lead to untold wealth.

The region was soon overwhelmed by waves of hopeful immigrants, some equipped with little more than tin spoons. These "Forty-niners," or "Argonauts" came by land and sea,

Below: Abilene in 1879. The corner building is constructed of brick in contrast to the false-fronted wooden buildings to the left.

Left: A miner with the tools of his trade; pick, shovel, and pan.

panning, and about twelve million ounces were recovered in this way. When this gold dried up, much harsher methods were used. Hydraulic mining began in 1853, on the Sierra's gravel-beds and hillsides. Although this was highly effective, and approximately eleven million ounces of gold were retrieved in this way, it was also extremely damaging to the environment. Streams and rivers were polluted by heavy metals, and huge quantities of silt were released into the environment. Most perilous of all, the forty-niners also mined gold in deep underground shafts. The precious metal was then extracted from its ore using highly toxic chemicals such as mercury and arsenic, which contaminated the land.

Another form of contamination, Asiatic cholera, swept the Plains in 1849., people of the local tribes also became

Right: The streams of the Sierra Nevada Mountains were rich with deposits of gold.

infected as did many immigrants and frontiers people.
Thousands died.

Violence against the Native Americans of the regions
increased greatly as the lust for gold became more intense
and widespread. Many miners attacked and killed the
indigenous peoples, feeling them to be in their way. The

Above: The methods of extracting gold were
extremely labor intensive and only one miner in
ten made any money from his efforts.

Above: Digging underground for gold was one of the most direct methods of obtaining the ore.

miners also decimated the area's wildlife, and many Indians starved for the lack of food.

While some of the early arrivals found gold, some of the later miners' journeys to "see the elephant" were a complete waste of time. Even successful miners were often forced to squander their "diggings" on simply surviving the super-heated inflation of the mining camps. Supplies, lodgings, and entertainment all came at spiraling prices, paid for in gold dust. A pound of sugar cost $2, a pound of coffee was $4, and a cooked meal could command as much as $25.

Unsurprisingly, the conditions in which the miners lived were extremely unhealthy. Most camped year round, and had very poor diets. With almost no medical care available, as many as 10,000 men succumbed to disease and malnutrition.

Some of the most successful men in the fold fields weren't miners at all, but suppliers. Californian Mormon Samuel Brannan was one of the first to profit from the miners. Brannan had triggered the initial gold hysteria in San Francisco, and opened a store right next to the original Sutter

dig. This soon developed into a chain stretching across the Californian gold fields. Brannan sold mining equipment and supplies, and made a fortune. Only` a few miners were so lucky. Most broke even or only lost. Many lost their health and the gold fields, and some lost their sanity. Many returned empty-handed to their homes in the East. Others stayed on in the West and took up other occupations, such as farming.

Several famous American entrepreneurs used the Gold Rush to kick-start their businesses. Levi Strauss sold jeans from a packhorse that he led through the mining camps. These were originally fashioned from brown canvas sailcloth, and were equipped with special gold ore storage pockets. Another famous company that had its roots in the gold fields was the meatpacking giant, Armour and Company. Philip Armour invested the small fortune he made from gold mining to start a wholesale grocery business in Wisconsin. This soon evolved into the Armour Company, which became the world's largest food processing business. Similarly, John Studebaker invested the $8,000 he had earned from selling wheelbarrows to the gold miners into his Studebaker Wagon Company. The rest, as they say, is history.

The city of San Francisco boomed, from a town of 500 souls in 1847, to one of 150,000 inhabitants in 1870. California became a state in 1850, and became increasingly important as it became wealthier. Many consider the state to be the home of classic American high-risk entrepreneurialism, perhaps of the American Dream itself. The demographic shift to the West also led to a concerted effort to connect the Pacific coast of America with the Eastern states. This, in turn, was the impetus behind better communications, such as the telegraph and the railroad.

The legend of the forty-niners has now been woven into the fabric of the Old West. They have also become a popular subject in American culture, beginning with Bret Harte's book of 1875, Tales of the Argonauts. Harte was a famous writer of Western stories, who evoked colorful life of the mining camps without ever having been there. Charlie Chaplin's 1925 film, The Gold Rush, exposes the hardships endured by the gold miners (viz. the famous image of the starving Little Tramp eating his own boot), but the movie is actually set in the gold fields of Alaska, rather than the Golden West.

Right: The city of San Francisco boomed from a town of 500 souls in 1847 to one of 150,000 in 1870.

WOMEN IN THE WEST
SAINTS IN SUN BONNETS AND NYMPHS DU PRAIRIE

"I am not so well satisfied with what I see of the women of the prairie cities… The ladies are all fashionably drest… their ambition evidently is to copy their eastern sisters. Something far different and in advance must appear, to tally and complete the superb masculinity of the West, and maintain and continue it."

Walt Whitman

"In all of the trying struggles of our nation, the women of America have borne a conspicuous part."

Abigail Scott Duniway

Right: Women enjoy their newfound liberation in the West.

Above: Woman drinking a beer in 1898.
Above left: Woman acrobat in various poses.

Although women formed a vital part of the waves of Westward immigration, men heavily outnumbered them in the years of the Old West. Unsurprisingly, this meant that females became a highly valued commodity among all types of male Westerners. The need to attract more women to the Frontier led to their position becoming increasingly advantageous, and many Western women enjoyed greater status and personal freedom than their Eastern counterparts. Utah was the first territory to enfranchise women, while California became the first state to legislate for married women to retain their property. In part, these legal differences in Western law reflected the tradition of the indigenous peoples but were also calculated to attract women of substance to the new territory.

While many women followed their men folk to the West, others made their own way to the Frontier. Others answered advertisements to go West as wives or female company. The prospect of adventure and greater autonomy appealed to many women, especially the more hardy and entrepreneurial. Once in the Wild West, these women had widely different experiences. Some became domestic goddesses, using their Eastern education and refinement to bring a touch of civilization to Frontier life. For them, Western life was often extremely tough. Their lives and those of their children were tenuous. Others adopted completely new, independent roles that defied the conventions of the time.

SALOON GIRLS AND SOILED DOVES

"The harlots, like the miners, wanted riches, and they joined in gold rushes from camp to camp, until too old and dirty and ugly to be desired by any but a sot, they killed themselves, or died in poverty alone."

Vardis Fischer and Opal Laurel Holmes in *Gold Rushes and Mining Camps in the Early American West*

It soon became apparent that Western morals were different. The Gold Rush in particular attracted a huge number of single men to the West, and they were soon in desperate need of "entertainment" and female company.

Left: Gathered round the kegs at Kelley's saloon, "The Bijou," at Round Pond, Oklahoma in 1894.

Below: Bader & Laubner's saloon at Dodge City in the 1880s, complete with polished bar and mirrors.

Right: Crapper Jack's
Dance Hall in Cripple
Creek, Colorado.

First came the miners to
Work in the mine,
Next came the ladies who
Lived on the line.

Old Western Mining Adage

Saloon and dance hall girls were virtually unknown in the East, but they became an integral and celebrated part of Western life. In most camps and Frontier towns, men outnumbered women three-to-one, but in the Gold Rush California of the 1850s, men formed ninety per cent of the population. Unsurprisingly, gold miners were notorious for their generosity to working girls. As the well-known prostitute Diamond Toothed Gerty remarked, "The poor ginks have just gotta spend it. They're that scared they'll die before they have it all out of the ground." Some miners were completely cleaned out by unscrupulous women and went back to the goldfields completely empty-handed.

Anxious to cash in on the booming economy of the West, saloon and dance hall owners lured attractive girls away from farms or mills. The more glamorous work they offered paid around $10 per week, plus commission on the over-priced drinks they sold to the customers. The girls dressed in brightly colored, ruffled dresses, with outrageously short skirts, net stockings and garters. More controversially, they also wore makeup, dyed their hair, and carried concealed weapons. But these "hostesses" were highly valued by the male customers, and many were lavishly rewarded for their company.

The West was soon thick with thousands of saloons. Most of these establishments sold their own particular concoction of "Firewater" whiskey, which might have contained raw alcohol, burnt sugar, chewing tobacco, turpentine, ammonia, gun power, and/or cayenne in its list of ingredients. Saloons also served warm beer.

Almost all saloons were hotbeds of gambling as well as vice. Among the professionals they attracted, such as Doc Holliday and Wild Bill Hickok, were a few female players. Perhaps the most famous of these was Lottie Deano, "The Queen of the Paste Board Flippers."

The first Western dance hall opened in 1849, and others opened almost immediately after. Most of the early customers were gold miners, who paid for their pleasures with pinches of gold dust. Men paid the equivalent of between 75 cents and a dollar for a dance ticket, which was split between the girls and the dance hall owners. Some girls danced up to fifty times a night and made small fortunes from this arduous toil. They were often paid in small ivory discs, which they redeemed for cash or gold dust at the end of the night. But these "hurdy girls" also received a great deal of unwanted attention, and over a hundred of them met violent deaths at the hands of their dance partners.

As well as these more innocent pleasures, a thriving sex industry also grew in the West. It is estimated that at least ninety per cent of the women in the mining camps were prostitutes. Many unprotected women, widows, and orphans were forced to turn to prostitution to support themselves, but others deliberately chose the profession. Some were looking for a nest egg to start a new life, while other women were

Left: Timberline, a noted Dodge City prostitute. She still displays some of the good looks she had before dissipation, drink, and disease ruined her and many other "soiled doves."

looking for a male protector. Others saw prostitution as a legitimate career in itself. As one Denver prostitute stated, "I went into the sporting life for business reasons and no other. It was a way for a woman in those days to make money and I made it."

The gold miners referred to these women as "ladies of the line" or "sporting women," while cowboys called them "soiled doves." Other euphemisms included "daughters of sin," "fallen frails," "doves of the roost," "scarlet ladies," "nymphs du prairie," "fair belles," "fallen angels," and less gallantly, "painted cats."

As the trade developed, a strictly hierarchical system of prostitution grew up. At the lowest level, single unprotected prostitutes worked the streets. These women were often alcoholics or drug addicts at the end of their careers. They carried blankets to lay down on the ground. These women plied their trade for a few coins, drink, or drugs. Slightly higher up the "professional" ladder were women who worked in the notorious

Above: A typical parlor girl, posed saucily, en dishabille.

"cribs." These were single, self-employed prostitutes working out of tiny, two-room apartments, which cost around $25 a week to rent. They charged between a quarter and two dollars for their services and entertained as many as sixty men each night. The forty-niners called streets made up of rows of cribs "the line." Sometimes, these women were on their way up in the profession and moved on to lower class brothels, or "cat houses." Women who stayed in the cribs had a life expectancy of only six years.

Brothels serviced a smaller and more affluent clientele and offered the girls a little more security and protection. The women in these establishments charged around $10 to $20 for a whole night of their time. Alternatively, the girls might set a ten-minute timer to entertain as many customers as possible.

At the top of the profession were the "parlor houses," and this was where the real money was made from prostitution. The "Madams" who ran these high-class brothels were often

accomplished businesswomen who became both rich and notorious. They attracted the best looking and most accomplished girls to their establishments and protected them as best as they could. Parlor house prostitutes often became courtesans, or mistresses, with their own particular clientele. Each had her own lavishly decorated bedroom, a large wardrobe of beautiful gowns, and a trunk for her savings. These fancy prostitutes paid their Madams for board and lodging, in a kind of cooperative business arrangement. For their part, the Madams paid off the police, kept "house" discipline, and served the ladies' clients with fine food and drink. The girls in these establishments generally charged around $20 to $30 for a night's company, but there were instances of girls being paid fabulous sums of money for their company. A generous gold miner gave the prostitute Julia Bulette no less than $1,000 to spend the night with him.

Prostitutes often hoped to return to a more "normal" way of life after a lucrative career and used colorful aliases to protect their identities, and the good name of their families. Dixie Lee was the most commonplace soubriquet for these "ladies of the lamp," but familiar nickname also included "Sweet Marie," "Ping Pong," "Timberline," and "Caprice." The "Spanish Queen," "Contrary Mary," and "Diamond Lil" were also famous prostitutes.

Although it was very difficult for prostitutes to make a fortune in the business of vice, some were able to graduate to being "Madams." Many of these women became highly successful. One famous Madam, Pearl de Vere, was reputed to charge her guests $250 per night at her exclusive establishment, "The Old Homestead," in Cripple Creek, Colorado. The notorious "Mammy Pleasant," also known as the "Lady of the Frontier," allegedly was the wealthiest woman in San Francisco. Other famous bordello proprietors included Fannie Porter of San Antonio, Dora Dufran of the Black Hills, Josephine Hensley of Montana, Mollie Johnson of

Above: Miss Laura's Brothel in Fort Smith, Arkansas has the rooms preserved and is now the town's tourist office.

Deadwood, and Laura Ziegler of Fort Smith, Arkansas. The first Oriental madam, Ah Toy, arrived in San Francisco in 1849. She coined the pidgin-English mantra "Two bittee lookee, fo bittee feelee, six bittee doee."

Several Western women from infamous criminal families also made their living in the sex trade. Pearl Starr, the daughter of the gun-slinging "Bandit Queen," Belle Starr,

founded a successful bordello in Fort Smith, Arkansas, while Wyatt Earp's sister-in-law, Besse Earp, became the most successful Madam in Wichita. Doc Holliday's hot-tempered girlfriend, "Big Nose" Kate, was also a notorious prostitute and, latterly, a brothel keeper.

Brothels soon became commonplace all over the West, springing up in every new Frontier town. There was even a floating barge brothel on the Belle Fourche River, which flows through Wyoming and South Dakota. The first "professional women" arrived in Deadwood in July 1876, including the rather unattractive-sounding "Dirty Em" and "Madam Mustachio." As Whitey Rupp, the owner of Wichita's famous Keno House brothel remarked, "The wages of sin are a darned sight better than the wages of virtue."

But the stark reality was that the lives of most prostitutes were desperate and unhappy. Abuse and violence were commonplace, and many workingwomen were kept as virtual sex slaves. Chinese, colored, and Native American women were particularly badly treated. Syphilis, consumption, and depression thrived among these fallen angels, and many turned to drugs and alcohol to ease their symptoms. The use of opium, laudanum, and morphine was common, and suicide virtually epidemic. Girls overdosed, shot themselves, swallowed strychnine, and used chloroform to end their misery. Early death became so commonplace that the life expectancy of a prostitute in the Old West has been estimated at around 23.1 years of age. Very few made it past thirty.

Despite this, prostitutes are now credited with an important role in the settling of the Frontier. Without them, many of the men who came to the West to make their fortunes would certainly have retraced their steps. Many of these brave girls also provided invaluable nursing services in the mining camps, saving many men from cholera and smallpox, with very little thought for their own safety. Despite this, as more "respectable" women came West, Western society became more critical of these "fallen women," as the Frontier gradually embraced the social mores of the East.

COWGIRLS

Nothing shows the more liberated attitude to Western women more clearly than the exciting life of the cowgirl. Tough but feminine, these real life Calamity Janes started by working family ranches when there weren't enough male hands. They became an integral part of Western life and have now gained a cult status.

The term "cowgirl" was invented to describe the extraordinary Lucille Mulhall. Lucille was the daughter of a wealthy Oklahoma ranch owner, Colonel Zach Mulhall. She was elegant and educated enough to be a society belle but preferred to practice her ranching skills, roping steers and

Above: A Montana cowgirl sits on her cow pony around the turn of the century.

Above: Stylishly posed cowgirl from 1902.

branding yearlings. Lucille was extremely skillful and became the top Western performer of the age, appearing at Madison Square Garden in 1905. The newspapers were at a complete loss to describe this original phenomenon. They dubbed Lucille the "Lassoer in Lingerie," "The Ranch Queen," and "The Female Conqueror of Beef and Horn." But they soon began to use the much neater and more accurate term of "cowgirl." Lucille was extraordinarily successful, topping vaudeville bills for over twenty years. Roy Rogers himself paid her an enormous compliment, describing her as the "World's greatest rider."

Back on the range, ordinary "hell raising" cowgirls shot, roped, and branded, while their more flamboyant counterparts starred in Western entertainments. Buffalo Bill Cody featured women rodeo riders in his Wild West Show from 1887. These girls scandalized many by wearing pants and riding astride their horses, while carrying pistols. Although Charles Goodnight had improved the original English design of the sidesaddle, it was completely impractical for working cattlewomen and feats of horsemanship.

Calamity Jane and Annie Oakley were two of the most famous women to join Cody's show. Annie was a backcountry orphan who became known as "Little Sure Shot." She was an extraordinarily able shot with a rifle or six-gun and married the exhibition marksman, Frank Butler.

The more eccentric Calamity Jane was born as Martha Jane Canary in Princeton, Missouri in 1852. "The White Devil of Yellowstone" was an extraordinary horsewoman who chewed tobacco and was handy with a rifle. Orphaned, and separated from her family from the age of fourteen, Martha Jane had had to make her own way in the world and chose to make it through the companionship of men. She became one of Buffalo Bill Cody's scouts, working for General Custer. She had extreme physical courage and saved several people from Indian attack, including a Captain Egan and a stagecoach full of passengers. Buffalo Bill accurately described Jane's life as being "pretty lively all the time." As well as scouting, she also worked as a "bullwhacker" in the mining camps and as a pony express rider on the dangerous trail between Deadwood and Custer. But Calamity also had a softer side, which she showed while helping to nurse the residents of Deadwood through a plague of smallpox. She became a local heroine for her tireless kindness.

Calamity met Wild Bill Hickok in 1876, and traveled with him for a while. Although it has often been assumed that the

Above: A studio shot of Calamity Jane.

pair had a romantic relationship, this must have been very brief, as Bill was shot dead later that year by "the assassin Jack McCall" (as it says on Hickok's tombstone). Calamity finally drank herself to death in 1903 and, at her own request, was buried next to Hickok in Deadwood cemetery. Also etched on his headstone is an appropriate motto, "We will meet in the happy hunting grounds to part no more."

Although the historical role of cowgirls is not as well documented as that of their male counterparts, their contribution to the taming of the West was considerable.

Above: "Cattle" Annie McDoulet and Jennie "Little Britches" Stevens.

Cattle Kate was another feisty Western women, whose real name was Ella Watson. Like Pearl Hart, Kate was divorced and thrown onto her own resources. She became a cattle rustler, increasing her herd by stealing her neighbors' animals. Less fortunate that Pearl, she was unlucky enough to become the only woman ever hanged in Wyoming, lynched by a vigilante mob of men who wanted her land.

Another famous pair of lady outlaws were the "Oklahoma Girl Bandits," "Cattle" Annie McDoulet and Jennie "Little Britches" Stevens. Stevens received her nickname for wearing large men's pants. Lookouts and messengers for the violent Doolin Gang, the girls were poor and uneducated teenagers who became crack shots under the tutelage of their criminal lovers. The pair was finally arrested for cattle rustling and selling bootlegged whiskey to the Indians. After brief prison sentences, the girls were released and reformed from their lives of crime.

Butch Cassidy's Wild Bunch was a large criminal gang that had several female associates. Most were drawn into crime through relationships with male gang members. Wild Bunch women included Etta Place, Laura Bullion, Annie Rogers, Rose Morgan, Maude Davis, and the Bassett sisters. These female bandits stole cattle and horses, robbed banks, fenced goods, laundered money, and held up trains across the West. Many had started out as prostitutes. Annie had worked at Fannie Porter's Sporting House in San Antonio, Texas, while Laura had been a dance hall girl from Sheridan, Wyoming.

Annie was Kid Curry's girl. Curry was the most dangerous and feared member of the Wild Bunch. They posed as man and wife and were finally captured as they tried to launder stolen money.

Laura started out with Will Carver, but when he was killed, she moved on to gang member Ben Kilpatrick. Together, they held up a Union Pacific train at Tipton, Wyoming, robbed the First National Bank in Winnemucca, Nevada, and held up another train (and stole $65,000) near Wagner, Montana.

Maud Davis and Rose Morgan were also female associates of the Wild Bunch but were unusual in that they were good Mormon women rather than ladies of ill repute. Both had children with gang members, but they were unable to get their husbands to reform.

Perhaps the West's most famous gangster's moll was Kate Elder, or "Big Nose Kate," as she is more popularly known. Kate led an extremely colorful life. She was born in Hungary

Their unique achievement is now celebrated in the Cowgirl Hall of Fame. Founded in 1975 in Hereford, Texas, the museum has now moved to Fort Worth.

FEMALE OUTLAWS AND WAYWARD CHARACTERS

Alongside its male villains, the Wild West also spawned several female outlaws. But far from being depraved desperadoes, almost all of these women turned to crime under the influence of men or through serious hardship. Although they adopted male behavior to become more or less successful thieves, very few women bandits were violent.

Pearl Hart holds the accolade of being the only woman known to have held up a stagecoach. Abandoned by her husband, Pearl was forced into crime by poverty. Captured at last, she used her feminine wiles to escape hanging and secure a reduced sentence.

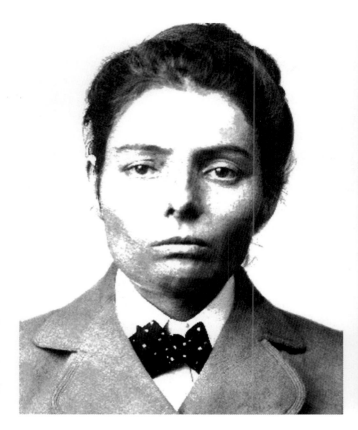

Above: Laura Bullion, who was involved with the Wild Bunch.

Above: "Big Nose" Kate, who had a volatile affair with Doc Holliday.

in 1850, but her family immigrated to Mexico in 1862, when her father was appointed as personal surgeon to Emperor Maximillian. As a young teenager, Kate ran away from home. She turned to prostitution after the death of her first husband, working in Bessie Earp's notorious "sporting house." Later, she became a dancing girl in Dodge City, before meeting Doc Holliday in 1878. The pair had an extremely volatile relationship, and even when they were a couple, Kate continued to work as a prostitute. The relationship finally floundered when she testified against Holliday in 1881, accusing him of being involved in a stagecoach robbery. Although she retracted her statement the next day, her disloyalty ended the relationship.

Another woman famously associated with a notorious criminal was the so-called "Rose of Cimarron." Her association with Dalton Gang member George "Bittercreek" Newcomb led to her being present at the West's most famous shootout. This took place in 1893, at Ingles in Oklahoma Territory, between the Dalton Gang and a posse of Deputy Marshals. The intense gunfire went on for over an hour, but Rose somehow managed to deliver a Winchester to her

Above: Rose of Cimarron, a well-known prostitute associated with the Dalton Gang.

sweetheart. "Rose" went on to expunge her youthful indiscretions by becoming the highly respectable wife of a senior Oklahoma politician.

Several other Western women refused to conform to their traditional roles and adopted the clothing and character of men. As a young girl, Charlie Parkhurst had adopted male attire to escape from an orphanage, but she retained her male identity as she grew up and became a professional stagecoach driver.

Similarly, the infamous Sally Skull masqueraded as a man to pursue her living as a horse trader. She simply would not have been taken seriously as a woman. However, Sally was also a sinister character who murdered several rivals to prosper her business.

Alice Ivers was another extraordinary character who chose to make her way in life by competing on equal terms in an all-male environment. A notorious professional gambler, "Poker Alice" was born in 1853 in Devonshire, England, and immigrated to Colorado with her family. Her first husband, Frank Duffield, taught her to play poker, and when he left her an unprotected widow, she began to gamble professionally. She was extremely successful and always carried a .38 revolver to defend her winnings, which could total $6,000 a night. Widowed three times, this colorful woman became a Deadwood legend and was buried in the Black Hills.

PIONEER WOMEN

Although they might have been somewhat less glamorous than other categories of Western females, pioneer women probably had the most positive impact on the region. Since Thomas Jefferson bought the Western states from the French, an increasing stream of American men and women made the "Great Migration" West across the Missouri. The trek became the greatest mass migration in American history. A steady flow of wagons, carts, and carriages left Pennsylvania, Virginia, Kentucky, and Tennessee to make the journey west. Over 350,000 pioneers had already passed over the Oregon, Santa Fe, and Mormon Trails before the first transcontinental railway route opened.

Women pioneers who trekked west came from many different backgrounds. Usually traveling with their husbands or fathers, these women came from the Eastern United States and European countries including England, Scotland, Germany, Scandinavia, and Spain. They had a variety of different motives and incentives for setting out on this arduous journey. Some, like the Quakers and Mormons, were looking for religious freedom. Others were farmers or cattlemen in search of land. According to English settler George Fromer, there was "good land dog-cheap everywhere." Under the Homestead Act of 1862, settlers were allowed to claim 160 acres for around $10, if they settled the land for at least five years. Others were sick of the urban poverty of their lives in the East and in the Old World, and they dreamed of a freer and healthier life in the West.

In 1865, Congress approved $85,000 to open up the wagon roads to the Rocky Mountains and the gold fields in the Dakota Territory. The Gold Rush was one of the greatest

Right: The Hancock Homestead at Sun River, Montana typified many of the new homes springing up in the West.

triggers to Western migration, motivating more than 80,000 people. It attracted all kinds of fortune hunters, desperados, adventurers, and failures, most of whom were single men. The miners then attracted hordes of "professional" women, including prostitutes and laundresses.

Very few women initiated the move to the West. Some were hardly consulted, while others actively begged their men folk to stay put. Many women, like Lavinia Porter, thought the trek would be a "wild goose chase." Usually, the women made the greatest sacrifices, leaving behind most of their goods and chattels and risking the lives of their children. But some preferred to stay with their husbands rather than be left as "Gold Rush widows." Women pioneers often oversaw the packing of the ox-drawn wagons that were to carry their families to the Frontier. Their aptitude for this crucial task could mean the difference between survival and death.

The many single women who went west, unaccompanied by male relatives, had their own motives for the trek. Some, like Narcissa Whitman and Kate Blaine, were missionaries, aiming to make religious converts in the "awfully wicked country" of the West. Others were businesswomen looking for opportunities. Widows and spinsters traveled west to find husbands. Some women were attracted by the greater personal freedom that the Western states offered. Women were allowed to retain their own property in several states, including Oregon, and several Western states gave women the vote.

The trek west became much more realistic for women travelers once stagecoach routes were established and the railroads opened up.

Right: A typical pioneer wagon. These conveyances enabled more women to accompany their men folk on the journey west.

Below: Women were a civilizing influence on the Western way of life.

Pioneer groups often fell into two categories, "stickers" and "movers." "Stickers" moved west in stages, even over several generations, or settled permanently along the route. "Movers" kept going until they reached the Frontier. Women pioneers did not necessarily make the decision to "move" or "stick" but made the best of the situation.

Before the railroads and stagecoaches, the trek itself was extremely difficult. Treasured personal possessions that had been packed with loving care were often discarded along the trail, and many women lost their children or husbands on the journey. Their pathetic graves were often marked only with unnamed headstones.

Even in the extremely difficult circumstances of the trail, women were still expected to discharge their "housekeeping" duties. Hampered by their long skirts and impractical equipment, the simplest task became extremely arduous. One women pioneer, Lodisa Frizzel, described how tough it was. "All our work here requires stooping. Not having tables, chairs, or anything. It is very hard on the back." Another traveler, Helen Carpenter, complained about the monotony of the trail diet. "One does like a change and about the only change we have from bread and bacon, is bacon and bread."

The harsh journey took its toll. Miriam Davis described

Above: The coming
of the stagecoach
made the West more
accessible to women.

Right: For many early
settlers, the journey to
the West proved fatal.

how she could hardly recognize herself at the end of it. "I have cooked so much in the sun and smoke that I hardly know who I am and when I look into the little looking glass I ask, 'Can this be me?'"

Once in the West, life did not get much easier. Many arriving pioneer women were shocked by the hardships they had to endure. Some women were obliged to keep house in very wild places. As soon as they arrived, the settlers had to build some kind of shelter and plant whatever crops they could. Sod houses were common as first Western homes, utilizing one of the prairie's few natural resources. Most early Frontier women not only had to look after the house and children, but were also expected to work alongside their men folk in the fields in an endless cycle of grinding labor. More educated women sometimes taught school or became midwives.

Under the Homestead Act, women of twenty-one years of

Above: A typical sod homestead.

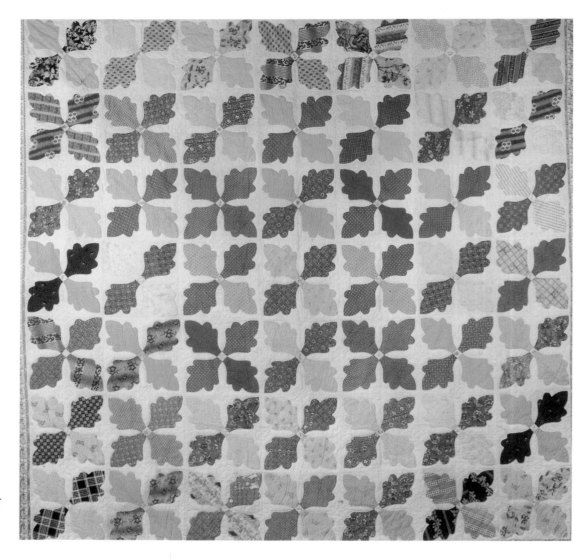

Right: Despite the drudgery, pioneer women found time for creative activities such as quilting.

age or over were also entitled to claim land, and by the end of the nineteenth century, almost twelve per cent of Western homesteaders were women. Some single women did all the physical work themselves or banded together with other women homesteaders. Despite the difficulties they faced, a greater proportion of female land claimants substantiated their claims than did male claimants. The ratio was 42 per cent of women, as opposed to 37 per cent of men.

Although there was a great deal of drudgery in the life of the Pioneer woman, many also found time for creativity. They quilted, sewed, and tended their flower gardens. Pioneer quilt blocks often celebrated the beauty of the prairie, with "log cabin," "bear's paw," and "pine tree" designs. They were also inspired by the journey West itself, as in the "wanderer's path," and "Oregon Trail" blocks.

Although their lives were physically challenging, it is said that Western women suffered from far fewer "nervous" diseases than their Eastern sisters. They greatly benefited from the lack of trivial social restraints and often formed wonderful friendships in their new home. Indeed, these "Madonnas of the Frontier" were critical in forging a new society in the West, providing the social glue that bound together small and vulnerable communities, and supporting their institutions, such as churches and schools. Marriage also welded these far-flung communities together, especially "sibling exchange" unions, when the children from one family married the children from another. This practice also kept family land claims together.

The hectic work schedule of Frontier women often reflected that of Caroline Ingalls, as set out by her daughter Laura in *Little House in the Big Woods.*

> *Wash on Monday*
> *Iron on Tuesday*
> *Mend on Wednesday*
> *Churn on Thursday*
> *Clean on Friday*
> *Bake on Saturday*
> *Rest on Sunday*

The hard work of these "Saints in sun bonnets" was essential to the survival of their families. Even more importantly, Pioneer women were often their children's only educators. They became the "ideal of all that is pure and ennobling and lovely here, her love is the light of the cabin home." These women were also the chroniclers of the early West and the life led by their families in the new territory. They wrote letters home and diaries detailing their experiences. One of the best-known female homesteaders is Elinore Pruitt Stewart, author of *Letters of a Woman Homesteader.*

Of course, some Pioneers, both male and female, didn't make it in the West and left empty-handed. Not everyone was equal to the tough life, and not all of the land grant parcels were workable. One dissatisfied settler carved his harrowing complaint on his cabin door, "30 miles to water, 20 miles to wood, 10 miles to hell and I've gone there for good."

Left: A recreation of Laura Ingalls's Little House on the Prairie.

The Grandest Enterprise Under God
The Transcontinental Railway

"May God continue the unity of our country, as the railroad unites the two great Oceans of the world."

Engraved on the final, Golden Spike

"I see over my own continent the Pacific railroad surmounting every barrier."

Walt Whitman

"You can lay track to the Garden of Eden, but what good is it if the only inhabitants are Adam and Eve?"

Head of the Northern Pacific Railway

"The Great Pacific Railway is commenced. Immigration will soon pour into these valleys. Ten millions of emigrants will settle in this golden land in twenty years… This is the grandest enterprise under God!"

George Francis Train

Right: Work begins on spanning the continent by rail.

The building of a transcontinental railway to unite the nation was proposed early in the nineteenth century. Ironically, it became a reality just as the nation was being torn apart by civil war. Abraham Lincoln signed the Pacific Railroad Act in 1862, which set out both the route of the line and how this huge enterprise was to be financed. Theodore Judah, the chief engineer of the Central Pacific Railroad, showed the long and complicated route to the President on a ninety-foot long map. Back in 1856, Judah had written a 13,000-word proposal to build the Pacific Railroad and became a lobbyist for the Pacific Railroad Convention.

The railroad was to have a huge impact on life in the West, opening it up to settlers. A dangerous trek that would have taken at least six months in the days of the wagon trains could now be accomplished in less than a week. But the obverse of this was the decimation of the bison, along with the complete loss of the unique Native American culture of the Great Plains.

The route of the transcontinental line followed the earlier trail routes and Pony Express trails. It was to run between Sacramento, California in the West and Council Bluffs, Iowa in the East, and was to pass through Nevada, Utah, Wyoming, and Nebraska en route. The railway did not actually reach the Pacific until 1869, when a new stretch of line was opened up to Oakland Point in San Francisco Bay. Nor was the line integrated into the Eastern railway system until 1872, with the opening of the Union Pacific Missouri

River Bridge. Its construction required tremendous engineering feats to overcome the obstacles of the route. The line crossed several rivers (including the Platte in Nebraska), the Rockies (at the Great Divide Basin in Wyoming), and the Sierra Mountains. Spur lines were to be built to service the two great cities of the Plains: Denver, Colorado, and Salt Lake City, Utah.

Unfortunately, another intrinsic characteristic of the development was to be corruption. The government legislated to award the constructors with 6,400 acres of trackside land, and a tiered payment per mile of track: $16,000 per mile for level track, $32,000 per mile for plateau track, and $48,000 for the most demanding stages. Within two years, these rates had been doubled. The investors were careful to ensure that as much track as possible was graded into the more expensive categories. The major inve a fortune in the Civil War by smuggling and stock speculation. Durant deviously tinkered with the route to ensure that it ran through his own property. Surveyor Peter Day said that "if the geography was a little larger, I think (Durant) would order a survey round the moon and a few of the fixed stars, to see if he could not get some depot grounds." Other investors like Oakes Ames were drawn into the Credit Mobilier scandal, where dummy contracts were awarded to Durant's own company. The scandal was to ruin their reputations and those of many other investors. Lincoln himself encouraged Ames to become involved in the enterprise, but it was to become his ruin. As railroad executive Charles Francis said, "It is very easy to speak of these men as thieves and speculators. But there was no human being, when the Union Pacific railroad was proposed, who regarded it as other than a wild-cat venture."

Union Pacific's corrupt investors became synonymous with the worst excesses of the so-called "Gilded Age." The term was coined by Mark Twain to describe the post-Civil War extravaganza of industrial-scale corruption when massive fortunes were made and lost. Many of the most magnificent San Francisco mansions were built with railroad money. The Panic of 1893 ended the Gilded Age abruptly. The financier Jay Gould replaced the discredited Durant at the head of Union Pacific and continued to steer the project.

The Central Pacific broke ground in January 1863 in Sacramento, California, while the Union Pacific waited until December that year to start work at Omaha, Nebraska. The groundbreaking ceremonies began a monumental task that was to take six years and involved the construction of 1,780

Previous page: A dramatic Currier and Ives 1870 print entitled "Through to the Pacific."

Right: Theodore D. Judah founded the Central Pacific and discovered the route over the Sierra Nevada Mountains.

Above: Union Pacific director, "Doc" Durant stands on the ties beyond the end of the advancing track in Nebraska, 1866.

Above: Construction locomotives near Bear River City, Wyoming.

miles of track. The varied difficulties and problems of the route meant that innovative engineering solutions were required. The trains of the day could not handle neither sharp curves nor an incline of more than two per cent, and the mountain ranges and canyons along the route were equally difficult to overcome. This enormous challenge required a massive workforce of over 100,000 men, who came from a wide variety of backgrounds. The majority were Irish-American veterans from both sides of the Civil War, together with Chinese immigrants, Mexicans, Englishmen, Germans, and ex-slaves from the South. Brigham Young also provided Mormon workers for the Utah sector of the line. These men were excellent, conscientious workers who ended each day of work with prayer and song rather than women and drink.

The project also required a wide array of tradesmen, surveyors, engineers, carpenters, masons, teamsters, tracklayers, telegraphers, spikers, bolters, and cooks. The work could be very dangerous. The use of early, unstable nitro-glycerin was particularly hazardous, and it resulted in many deaths and injuries. The crews from the two railroad companies were under strong competitive pressure to complete as many miles of track as possible, and their work often became sub-standard. The railway companies were paid per mile of track, not for the durability of

their construction, so their priority was to get the job done as quickly as possible. Slick track laying teams laid as many as four rails per minute. Ultimately, the Union Pacific was to build about two-thirds of the track.

Anxious not to lose a minute of working time, the railroad companies housed thousands of workers in enormous work-trains. These had sleeping cars outfitted with three-tier bunk beds, kitchens, and eating cars. The life for these men was extremely hard, and the pay, meager. There were several strikes, particularly among the less well-paid Chinese workers, but the companies were ruthless employers.

The two ends of the Pacific line moved slowly together and

Above: Surveyors formed the first workforce. They endured many hardships, sleeping on the ground and fearing Indian attack.

further into the wilderness. The workforce was spread out over several miles and was accommodated in mobile tent towns that followed the route. The end-of-line boomtowns that were created were colorful and lawless. They included North Platte, Julesburg, Abilene, Bear River, Wichita, and Dodge. The final tent town, Corinne, Utah, was founded in January 1869. These camps became known as "Hell on Wheels," as they were full of vice and criminality and were rough, bawdy, and brutal. Newspaper editor, Samuel Bowles, coined the term and described their inhabitants as the "vilest men and women… (a) congregation of scum and

wickedness… by day disgusting, by night dangerous. Almost everybody dirty, many filthy, and with the marks of lowest vice; averaging a murder a day; gambling, drinking, hurdy-gurdy dancing and the vilest of sexual commerce."

In reality, the tent towns were indeed conurbations of saloons, gambling houses, dance halls, and brothels. Almost all the women living in these settlements were prostitutes. Murder, arson, and violent crime were rife. Without any real law enforcement, frontier justice was the only control, and lynching was common. John Ford captured the decadent atmosphere of Hell on Wheels in his 1924 silent film, *The*

Above: A banner celebrating reaching Cozad, Nebraska, 247 miles from Omaha.

Right: Union Pacific locomotive Number 82 and its crew. Photographed in 1872, between Echo, Utah and Evanston.

Left: The Central Pacific and Union Pacific railroads meet on May 10, 1869.

Below: Chinese workers were mainly responsible for constructing the Central Pacific Track. They lived in tents along the line.

Iron Horse. Although the film was not entirely accurate, Ford also showed the spirit of fervent nationalism that drove the project. Despite their inauspicious beginnings, many of these tent towns became permanent settlements. Mark Twain described the gold rush and end-of-the-line rail town at Sacramento as being no more than a "city of saloons," but it was soon to become the state capital of California.

The railroad companies actively encouraged immigration, from both China and Europe. The Chinese population in particular grew exponentially, from less than a hundred people in 1870, to over 140,00 men and women in 1880.

Above: Corinne, Utah was the final tent town of a whole string of colorful and lawless places along the construction route.

Left: The Governor Stanford, the first of Central Pacific's twenty-three locomotives, on its way to the joining of the rails celebrations.

The companies employed agents to scout for immigrants, who were paid per head. C. B. Schmidt was the champion of scouts, responsible for settling over 60,000 German immigrants along the route of the Santa Fe Railroad. Settlement of the prairie led to a massive increase in American farming. The two million working farms that existed in 1860 had grown to six million by the end of the century.

Unfortunately this colossal increase in white settlement was one great source of anger to the Native American peoples of the Plains. The other was the decimation of the American Bison, or buffalo. This animal was unique to the Plains, and before the railroad, it was estimated that as many as sixty million animals roamed the prairie in massive herds. The buffalo was crucial to the existence of the Plains Indians and had a special spiritual significance to them. "Everything the Kiowas had had come from the buffalo," said tribe member Old Lady Horse, "Their tipis were made of buffalo hides, so were their clothes and moccasins. They ate buffalo meat." The other Plains tribes, including the Cheyenne, Lakota, and Apache, were equally dependant on the buffalo.

In complete contrast, the railway companies saw the ancient bison herds as a nuisance, useful only for the feeding of their workforce. They hired buffalo hunters to wipe them out, the most famous being Buffalo Bill, who rode forth with his horse, Buckskin, and his gun, Lucretia. He alone shot over four thousand animals and organized many hunting expeditions. Later, the railroad encouraged "hunters" to shoot buffalo from specially adapted railcars to minimize any risk

or inconvenience. Elisabeth Custer described how "the wild rush to the windows, and the reckless discharge of rifles and pistols put every passenger's life in jeopardy." This trend became so widespread that the Kansas Pacific Railroad ran its own taxidermy service to mount trophies for their customers. The upshot of this dreadful slaughter was that, by the end of the end of the nineteenth century, only a pathetic remnant of fewer than a thousand animals remained from the majestic herds that had dominated Plains life for centuries.

Seeing their way of life being destroyed before their eyes, some of the more warlike Plains Indian tribes began to organize scouting parties to vandalize trains and attack surveyors and other railway workers. This gave the rail companies the excuse they needed to strike back. According to General Grenville Mellen Dodge, the chief engineer of the Union Pacific, "We've got to clean the damn Indians out, or give up building the Union Pacific Railroad." The Sand Creek Massacre of November 1864 was one of the most appalling incidents that took place, when men of the Colorado Territory militia destroyed a village of Cheyenne and Arapaho, killing over two hundred elderly men, women, and children. Although the massacre was widely condemned, no one was brought to justice. Sand Creek led to a series of revenge killings in the Platte Valley, and over two hundred innocent white settlers were murdered. The increasing spiral of violence made it progressively more difficult for an accommodation to be found between the Plains natives and the railroad companies. The regular U.S. Cavalry was deployed to protect the security of the trains, and Dodge ordered the Powder Ridge Expedition of 1865, in which his forces rode against the Lakota, Cheyenne, and Arapaho. Although this was partly successful, hostilities soon escalated into the Reds Clouds War, fought against the Lakota tribe in 1866. The Lakota braves inflicted heavy casualties, and it was the worst defeat that the U.S. Cavalry was to suffer until Little Big Horn, ten years later.

Their resistance to the railroad led to Plains tribes being confined in reservations, where they were powerless to protect their ancestral hunting grounds, or the buffalo.

On May 10, 1869, the Central Pacific and Union Pacific tracks finally met at Promontory Summit, Utah. Leland Stanford, the Governor of California and one of the "big four" investors in the Central Pacific, drove home the final, golden spike that joined the two lines. This was one of the world's first global media events, as both hammer and spike were wired to the telegraph line, and Stanford's ringing blows were simultaneously broadcast to the East and West Coasts of America.

The line had a great impact on the whole country, but its effects were most directly felt in the West. It proved to be a major stimulus to immigration and trade within the region. Soon, other railroads crisscrossed the Plains, including the Kansas Pacific, North Pacific, Denver Pacific, Texas and Pacific, Burlington and Missouri River, Denver and Rio Grande, Atchison, Topeka, and Santa Fe railroads. By 1876, it was possible to travel between New York and San Francisco in 83 hours and 39 minutes.

This extraordinary achievement went on to be celebrated as an iconic element of Western culture. The railroad is familiar from any number of movies, as the great iron horses drive over the monumental Western landscape. In 1936, Cecil B. DeMille released *Union Pacific*, which explored the corruption that surrounded the building of the line. 196s's epic movie, *How the West Was Won*, also dealt with the dramatic construction of the Union Pacific line, especially with how the railroad bosses drew the rage of the Native American tribes on their workers, and how the Cavalry attempted to protect them. One of the film's most famous scenes is of a herd of buffalo stampeding across the railroad.

The Union Pacific left a permanent mark on American life in both the East and West. The line itself has been renewed many times, but much of it is still laid on the original, hand-prepared grade. In several places, where later routes have bypassed the initial line, it is still possible to see the original track, abandoned in the wilderness.

Above: The Great Event poster announces the staggering achievement of a railroad from the Atlantic to the Pacific, serving "Travelers for Pleasure, Health, or Business."

WESTERN TOWNS

The look and feel of Old Western towns is so completely familiar to us that we can easily imagine walking down the dusty boardwalk, and through a pair of swing doors into the saloon. The classic frontier town looks flimsy, like an ephemeral movie set, and the insubstantial, flat-fronted buildings have a wonderful cinematic quality. They usually started as one-street towns, with hitching rails in front of the buildings. This thoroughfare would be lined with archetypal Western institutions: saloons, trading posts, sheriffs' offices, livery stables, banks, gunsmiths, and telegraph offices. As they became more established, a Wells Fargo Office, a Texas Rangers' office, newspaper office, barbershop, town jail, apothecary, dentist, photographer, or hotel might also have opened for business. Many towns also catered for the more spiritual side of life, by establishing a church, and every town of the Old West required its own cemetery.

Right: Texas Rangers discuss tactics.

Thousands of Western towns sprang up as frontier life developed. They grew up at railheads, along cattle trails, near gold fields and silver mines, and around military forts. They were often isolated and surrounded by miles of empty, threatening wilderness. Western civilization was completely different that than of the East. The landscape was bigger, and the towns were smaller.

The early establishment of law and order was crucial to the development of these towns from shiftless camps into permanent settlements. Where this proved impossible, towns were often abandoned. Towns whose water or gold ran out and towns bypassed by the railroads or cattle trails shared this ignominious fate.

Life in the Old West was extremely volatile, and new arrivals searched about restlessly, looking for land and opportunity. Many new towns were founded, and abandoned a few years later.

Giving up Drinking is the easiest thing in the world. I know because I've done it thousands of times.

Mark Twain

The saloon was often the first building in a Western town, and might start out as just a tent or lean-to. When it became more permanent, it might also be used as a public meetinghouse. Brown's Hole near the Wyoming-Colorado-Utah border was the first drinking house to become known as a saloon, back in 1822, and catered for the region's fur trappers. A town often had more than one saloon, often completely disproportionate to its population. Livingston, Montana, for example, had a population of only 3,000, but no fewer than 33 saloons. Saloons often served liquor (whiskey, bourbon, rye, and beer) twenty-four hours a day, and their clientele reflected a cross-section of the West's white male population. These men included cowboys, gunmen, lawmen, and gamblers. Women,

Above: The St. James' Saloon in Dodge City is typical of Western bars of the period.

Previous page: Abilene, Kansas looking south from 3rd and Cedar, around 1882.

Above: Every early Western town had a covered well.

Left: Wichita, Kansas consisted of false-fronted wooden structures in 1871.

Chinese, and black Americans were unwelcome, while it was actually illegal for Indians to enter. Of course, the barring of women did not extend to the saloon girls who worked in the establishments, selling over-priced drinks to the customers, and keeping them company. Surprisingly, very few of these women were prostitutes.

Many saloon proprietors were criminals and gunmen, in the same way that many wayward women ran bordellos. These included Wyatt Earp, Bob Ford (Jesse James's killer), Doc Holliday, and Wild Bill Hickok.

As the West became more sophisticated, saloons offered a variety of entertainment including fine dining, billiards, singing, dancing, and bowling. But the primary saloon pastimes were drinking and gambling. Almost every saloon had a poker table and spittoons, and many different card games were played. Of course, gaming often led to violence, which regularly spilled out on to the street. A complex "bar etiquette" also prevailed, which governed the buying and accepting of drinks. Breeches of this unwritten code could also lead to serious trouble.

Equally important to every town was its general store, or trading post. Without it, it would be almost impossible for a town to get off the ground. It has often been remarked that some of the biggest fortunes made in the Old West were

made, not by miners or settlers, but by the tradesmen who supplied them. As Louis L'Amour's character Newt Clyde says of Gage, Confusion's nervous storekeeper, "When he leaves, the town is finished." Depending on their location, the general store would stock farm supplies, mining equipment, or cowboy gear. They also carried basic foodstuffs and seeds to get the "sodbuster" farmers started, while they removed the prairie turf to plant their crops. The general store would also supply the townsfolk with their basic needs. Perhaps the most famous Western store in popular culture is the Olesons' general store in Laura Ingalls Wilder's hometown of Walnut Grove, Minnesota. The Olesons' ambiguous social status is also interesting. While storekeepers were vital to the development of the West, many used their virtual monopolies

Above: As the age of advertising began, many advertisements were produced locally.

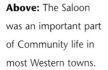

Above: The Saloon was an important part of Community life in most Western towns.

to charge extortionate prices. General stores and trading posts were also great social centers, where news and gossip were exchanged.

After a few years of manic prosperity, many Western towns simply disappeared from the map. The region is scattered with ghostly, abandoned towns, many of whose eerie streets have not heard a footstep, or a hoof beat, for years.

Left: An elaborate Whiskey decanter dating from the 1880s.

Left: J. Muellers Shop in Ellsworth, Kansas, photographed for posterity in 1872.

Right: The Church formed an important community meeting place.

Below: Hotels reflected the increased mobility of Western life due to the advent of the stagecoach and the railroads.

Above: The Western Union telegraph service dated from 1856. It linked the Atlantic and Pacific coasts in 1871.

Above: Small local businesses, like gunsmiths, were established to service the surrounding area.

Above: No town was above the law. The United States Marshals Service saw to that.

Above: Many towns owed their existence and livelihood to the mining trade.

Above: As towns grew more prosperous it was important to provide a bank where worthy citizens could safely keep their money.

Right: The Western General Store kept all manner of goods brought from back East by the new railroad.

Above: In new territories agents were appointed so that settlers could stake their claims.

Above: All towns needed a cemetery. Some needed them more than others.

SODBUSTERS, LOG CABINS, AND FRAMES

✶   ✶   ✶   ✶   ✶   ✶

Although our image of a prairie home tends to consist of a romantic log cabin in the style of the *Little House on the Prairie*, the lack of indigenous timber and other building materials meant that early frontier settlers were obliged to build more organic structures.

Right: Log homes provided quick and flexible accommodation.

Left: Logs provided a raw material for huts and shelters of all kinds. Some early towns were entirely constructed from logs.

Above: Early settlers were known as "sodbusters." They literally broke up the surface of the virgin prairie with their plows. John Deere made his name by designing the first non-sticking plow. It turned the heavy prairie soil into a fertile growing medium.

Sodbusters earned their name by becoming the first farmers to disturb the grassland of the Great Prairie; the first to plow the open wilderness. They also built a very special kind of home that became a nickname for the prairie-dwellers later. These early prairie dwellings were made from the virgin turf of the Great Plains itself. Some of these "sodbusters" were built into banks and hillsides, "dug in like coyotes," as one woman homesteader described it, but others were freestanding.

In the construction of these unusual homesteads, only the window frames and doors were made using timber. The walls were raised with buffalo grass sods, which were also used to cover the roof. The sods were strips of prairie turf, of between twelve to eighteen inches wide, and eighteen inches long. They were usually around three inches deep. They were laid in double rows for greater strength. Even the newcomers' chicken houses were built with these materials. Many settlers also built a "cave" to keep their provisions cool in summer, and stop them from freezing in winter. This was particularly important in an area whose daily temperature fluctuates between minus 30 and 110 degrees Fahrenheit. The sod homesteads were also thermally efficient, and could be very comfortable.

With an annual rainfall of just fifteen inches, it was very

Above: The interior of a log cabin, with old timers gathered round the fire.

hard to grow grain on the prairie, and the sodbusters' 160-acre plots provided enough grazing for only eight cows. Despite this, many settlers fell in love with the wonderful landscape of the Badlands, and their peaceful lives there, with just prairie dogs and gophers for company.

Sod homes may have been the first residences of the new settlers, but the coming of the railroad meant that conventional building materials could be shipped into the area. At this time, many sodbusters were replaced by log cabins. But timber remained a scare and expensive resource on the virtually treeless plains. Homesteaders still had to haul logs for many miles from railheads, or from isolated groves of hardwood trees.

Settlers that managed to acquire enough elm and cottonwood logs used them to build extremely practical and adaptable structures, which could be extended when necessary. The logs were notched at the corners to make rigid boxes, and "chinking" between the logs provided insulation. The chinking consisted of thin strips of wood which were pushed into the gaps between the logs and covered with a daub of earth and prairie grass. Cabin roofs were made from hand-split red oak or cedar shakes. Some of these log cabins were even whitewashed. But the continued scarcity of materials meant that most prairie cabins were much smaller than those in other areas. Typically, they measured just sixteen by eighteen feet, and were built facing south, to catch the warmth of the sun.

The on-going timber shortage ensured the popularity of the next building method introduced to the plains: framing. Frame homes used far less wood than log cabins, and were both sturdier and more weather proof. They were also simple to build, as they required no foundations, and they proved to be extremely durable.

Plains homes representative of all three building methods survive today, and many have been preserved. Others are still occupied, giving shelter to modern plainsmen and women.

Above: This family's shelter is roofed with turfs of prairie grass.

Boomers, Sooners, and Moonshiners

O ver a period of less that a century, the rush to settle the West meant that only a few areas of virgin land remained by the mid-1880s. By this time, the Indian Territory had become the final Frontier. Although more than fifty-five Native American tribes occupied parts of this designated territory, which lay to the west of the Mississippi, the vast majority of the land was uninhabited. This huge area was called the Oklahoma District. *Harper's Weekly* described it as "The last barrier of savagery in the United States."

Right: The Claims Office at Round Pond, Oklahoma Territory in January 1894.

J. W. CRAIG
SURVEYOR & LOCATER

A. M. MACKEY
ATTORNEY at LAW

U.S. LAND OFFICE PRACTICE
CONTESTS a SPECIALTY

President Benjamin Harrison proclaimed the area open to settlement in the Indian Appropriations Act of March 2, 1889. The Act stated that any settler could claim 160 acres of public land. The Army became involved, clearing the land of illegal squatters, and organized the first great land run on April 22, 1889. This was supposed to give every settler an equal opportunity to claim the best land of the Oklahoma District. As the bugles blew at precisely noon on that day, over 100,000 "Boomers" cycled, rode trains, and drove wagons into the territory. Unfortunately, these fair-minded individuals were often pre-empted by the so-called "Sooners," who had already sneaked into the Oklahoma District and claimed many of the best plots. The unscrupulous Sooners were often deputy marshals, surveyors, or railroad workers whose work had given them access to the District, and an opportunity to study the land.

A third category of settlers, the "Moonshiners" had also jumped the gun, sneaking through the lines of soldiers to get onto the territory by the light of the moon.

By nightfall on April 22, an amazing 1.92 million acres of

the "Unassigned Lands" had been claimed. At the same time, Guthrie, which was to become Oklahoma's first state capital, was already a tent city of 15,000 souls. Within five days of the land run, the first wooden buildings were already being raised in the town. By September that year, Guthrie had three newspapers, a hotel, three general stores, and fifty saloons.

Across the territory, everything necessary for civilized life sprang up almost at once. Tradesmen established their businesses, and three men set up a bank with money they had printed themselves. They used a potbellied stove as their

Below: The Boomer's Camp at Arkansas City, Kansas. The occupants were waiting for the strip to open March 1, 1893.

Above: The first blacksmith shop in Guthrie, Oklahoma Territory, circa 1889.

Above: The clerical workers of the U.S. Land Office of Perry, Oklahoma Territory, photographed with the local U.S. Deputy Marshals on October 12, 1893.

Right: The Wild West Hotel, Calamity Avenue, Perry, Oklahoma Territory, photographed in September 1893.

Above: W.H. McCoy's claim, Perry, Oklahoma Territory, October 1, 1893.

Above: Temporary bank buildings and the beginnings of a lodging house in Perry, Oklahoma Territory.

Right: Hell's Half Acre, Perry, Oklahoma Territory, taken in 1893.

vault.

Within weeks, the Oklahoma District was scattered with embryonic new cities, including Oklahoma City, Stillwater, Norman, and Kingfisher.

Under the Organic Act of 1890, the Oklahoma District became the Oklahoma Territory. Further land rushes opened up more and more land to settlement, although most of these were done by ballot. The largest took place in 1893, when the six-million-acre Cherokee Outlet was distributed among 100,000 new settlers.

It was not until November 16, 1907 that Oklahoma became a state in its own right, when President Theodore Roosevelt signed a proclamation to that effect.

In the early twentieth century, the discovery of "black gold" in Oklahoma led to a great influx of wealth into the state, and many of Oklahoma's most prestigious families made their fortunes at this time.

THE OLD WEST IN POPULAR CULTURE

 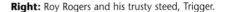

Arguably, the first Western writer was James Fennimore Cooper, whose *Leatherstocking Tales* were first published between 1827 and 1841. These included his iconic story, "The Last of the Mohicans." Cooper's tales featured his hero Natty Bumppo, or Hawkeye, who was based on real life characters such as David Shipman, and the pioneer Thomas Leffingwell.

But the invention of classic Western fiction as we understand it today dates from the Civil War. Its introduction marked the beginning of an almost universal fascination with the Old West, which was to have a huge impact on our culture. Almost immediately, this first Western writing set out the themes that were to dominate the genre. These included death, the barren landscape, horseflesh, hard men, marginalized women, and Indians. It was set in the Old West of the nineteenth century, and often deals with the repercussions of the Civil War. This traditional subject matter is still current, but has also been subverted and embellished to create many Western sub-genres.

Right: Roy Rogers and his trusty steed, Trigger.

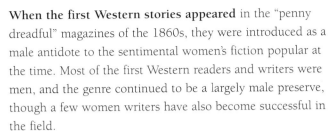

Above: A Western half-dime novel from the Beadle Library.

When the first Western stories appeared in the "penny dreadful" magazines of the 1860s, they were introduced as a male antidote to the sentimental women's fiction popular at the time. Most of the first Western readers and writers were men, and the genre continued to be a largely male preserve, though a few women writers have also become successful in the field.

Around 1860, Western dime novels succeeded the penny dreadfuls, and these survived into the 1940s. The first of these was *Maleaska, the Indian Wife of the White Hunter.* Ironically, a woman, Ann Sophia Stephens, wrote the story and she is credited with the invention of this popular literary form.

America became increasingly literate after the Civil War, and cheap and accessible dime novels became very popular. They were often produced with salmon colored paper

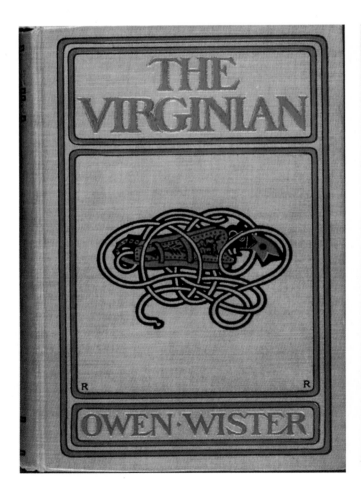

Above: *The Virginian* was published in 1902.

Above: An early dime novel with a lurid jacket.

wrappers. Dime Westerns often featured real-life heroes such as Buffalo Bill, Kit Carson, Billy the Kid, and Jesse James. These stories became increasingly formulaic, with cool, detached heroes, resourceful cowboys, pure heroines, outlaw bands, Indians, violence, and gunplay.

Owen Wister's more literary Western novel, *The Virginian*, was published in 1902, and became the first classic Western. Wister made his first trip to Wyoming in 1885, and became a close friend of the Western artist Frederic Remington. His book was a highly mythologized version of the Johnson County War.

Hopalong Cassidy, Clarence E. Mulford's famous cowboy character, first appeared in 1904. Cassidy was to become the inspiration for no less than sixty-six movies as well as radio and television series.

Zane Grey's first novels also appeared in the early years of the twentieth century. He published *Heritage of the Desert* in 1910, and *Riders of the Purple Sage* in 1912. An East Coast dentist, Grey wrote over ninety Western novels, and became one of the first celebrity millionaire Western writers. His stories are set in the classic Western landscape of Utah, Arizona, Northern Mexico, and Colorado, and feature noble cowboy heroes. Zane's success popularized the legend of the Old West across the country.

Another Western author from the early 1900s was Andy Adams, who wrote the Log of a Cowboy, published in 1903, the story of a five-month, 3,000-mile cattle drive along the Great Western Cattle Trail.

Adams's publishing contemporary, Frank Hamilton Spearman, was born in 1859. He published his first Western title, the *Nerve of Foley*, in 1900, and his 1906 book, *The Whispering Smith*, was made into no fewer than three films in

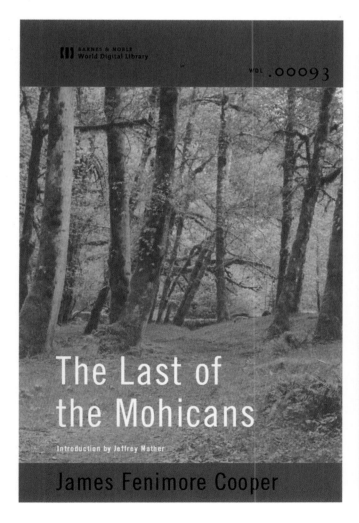

Above: *The Last of the Mohicans* was first published in 1826.

Above: Hopalong Cassidy first appeared in 1904.

Above: Zane Grey wrote over ninety Western novels.

Right: *Whispering Smith* was made into no fewer than three films.

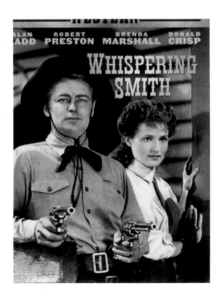

1915, 1925, and 1947.

In 1919, Street and Smith published the first Western story magazine. This format also found a niche, and survives today. Western story magazines launched the writing careers of several prominent writers in the field, including that of Louis L'Amour, the "Laureate of the Lariat."

Another writer who began by writing for "pulp" magazines, and the later "slicks," was the Western fiction writer Max Brand. Brand (born Frederick Schiller Faust) invented the famous Western character "Destry." He went on to write over five hundred stories and movie scripts for Warner Brothers.

Several pulp writers went on to publish popular Western novels. The popularity of these inexpensive publications exploded in the 1920s and 1930s, and many famous Western novels date from this period.

An explosion of movies inspired by the Old West paralleled the popularity of Western writing, and many were filmed in the 1920s.

J. Frank Dobie, the famous Texan plainsman, also published his first book in this decade. *A Vaquero of the Brush Country* appeared in 1929. His final work, *The Mustangs*, appeared in 1952. This highly realistic Western writing influenced the genre for many years.

Another "real-life Westerner," journalist and trapper Luke Short, began to publish Western fiction in the 1930s and his book, *The Feud at Single Shot*, was published in 1935. One of the most dominant Western novelists of the 1950s, he published over forty further titles until his final novel, *Trouble Country,* appeared in 1976.

The paperback novel was the most successful form of Western publishing in the 1940s, and many of the most celebrated stories of this genre date from this decade. These include *The Ox-Bow Incident* by Walter Vantilburg Clark (1940), A. B. Guthrie's *The Big Sky* (1947) and *The Way West* and *Shane* (both 1949), by Jack Schaefer.

Tom W. Blackburn also began his writing career in the 1940s with the publication of *Tumbleweed with Spurs* (1940), the first of a series of Western novels. Perhaps his most famous achievement was the lyrics he wrote for the *Ballad of Davy Crockett*, which introduced the famous 1955 television series. Blackburn also contributed scripts to television shows such as *Maverick, Daniel Boone*, and *The Virginian*.

Blackburn's literary contemporary, A. B. "Bud" Guthrie, was another prize-winning author who wrote and published many Western novels. His career began in the early 1940's, and he continued to publish until 1982. In 1950, Guthrie won the Pulitzer Prize for *The Way Out West*.

Novelist Jack Schaefer also began his illustrious career in this decade, with the publication of *Shane* in 1949. The book was made into a movie and two television series. Schaefer continued to publish Western stories until the 1980s.

The 1950s saw an extensive flourishing of Western writing and publishing, and several notable literary careers were launched.

Elmer Kelton was a hugely successful Western writer, whose career peaked in the 1950s. Among his most popular novels were *Barbed Wire* and *Buffalo Wagons,* both of which appeared in 1957. Famous as a "Texas Legend," Kelton was voted the Best Western Author of All Time by The Western Writers of America (an organization founded in 1953). Kelton's books have also won their annual Spur award on seven occasions.

Willis Todhunter Ballard also wrote thousands of short stories and over fifty film and television scripts in the 1950s, all in the Western genre. His book *The Circle C Feud* was published in 1952.

The 1950's also saw the launch of Louis L'Amour's highly successful career, with the publication of his first Western title, *Westward the Tide* in 1950. L'Amour went on to dominate Western writing for several decades, inspiring many movies and television shows, until the publication of his final work, *The Haunted Mesa,* in 1987. L'Amour drew on his experiences to write over a hundred novels, and went on to sell over 225 million books.

By contrast, Elmore Leonard was an educated graduate of the University of Detroit. But like L'Amour, Leonard's Western writing career began with short stories. The pulp magazine *Argosy* used his first effort, "The Trail of the Apache," in 1951. Leonard's first Western novel, *The Bounty Hunters,* appeared in 1953, and he soon became known for his gritty and realistic style. He went on to publish a long list of titles, including *Hombre* in 1961, *Bandits* in 1989, and *Get Shorty* in 1990.

Giles A. Lutz, was another prolific writer of Western novels and short stories in this period. Lutz went on to write several well-known books, including *A Drifting Man, The Honyocker,* and *Smash The Wild Bunch.*

Lauran Paine was another productive writer. Born in 1916, he launched his first Western novel, *Arrowhead River,* in 1956, and went on to publish over a hundred books under several pseudonyms. His work was also made into two

Above: One of over forty titles written by Luke Short.

Left: Luke Short's real name was Frederick Dilley Glidden. He took his penname from the famous Western gunslinger, pictured here.

Above: *The Big Sky* is set in Montana in the early 1800s.

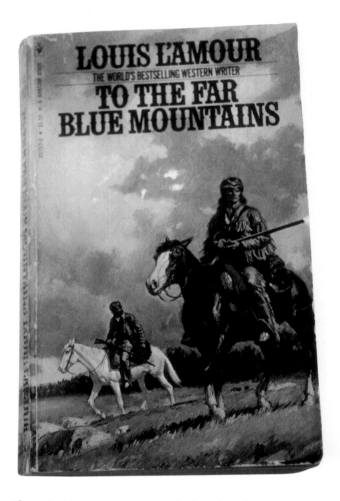

Above: Louis L'Amour wrote extensively about the early settlers.

movies, *The Quiet Gun* in 1957 (based on his novel *Law Man*), and *Open Range* in 2003.

Paine's contemporary and writer of Western fiction, Louis B. Patten, published his first novel, *The Snake Stomper* in 1951, and went on to write over ninety titles in this genre. His last was *Track of the Hunter*, published in 1981. In 1979, Patten won the Western Writers of America Saddleman Award for his "outstanding contribution to the American West."

The 1950s also saw the launch of Larry McMurty's career. McMurty is best known for his 1985 novel, *Lonesome Dove*. The book told the story of a cattle drive between Texas and Montana, and won the 1986 Pulitzer Prize for fiction. It was also the inspiration behind the 1990s television series.

J. T. (John Thomas) Edson, whose career also took off in

the 1950s, was something of a rarity among Western writers. He was an Englishman, born in Derbyshire, who had never visited America. Despite this, Edson wrote over a hundred Western titles, drawn solely from his imagination. Edson's technique was like that of East Coast dentist Zane Grey, who also had no experience of the frontier. Despite this, Edson's books were hugely successful, selling over 11 million copies.

The 1960s was another successful decade for Western writing. The popularity of the genre was greatly stimulated by the many Western television series, including NBC's number one rated show *Bonanza*.

The 1970s saw two female writers gaining success in the Western genre. Lee Hoffman published seventeen novels between 1966 and 1977, and her 1967 novel *The Valdez Horses* won the Western Writers of America Spur Award. Dorothy Marie Johnson had also won this award for her 1956 short story, "Lost Sister." She published two important frontier novels in the 1970s, *Buffalo Women* and *All the Buffalo*

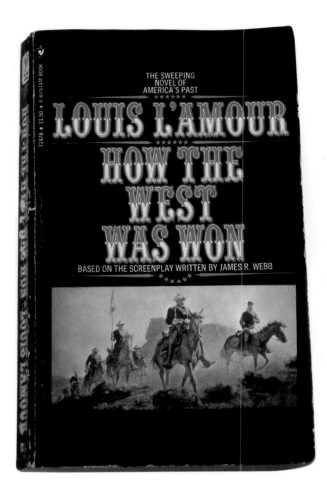

Above: : L'Amour's epic novel of Western expansion.

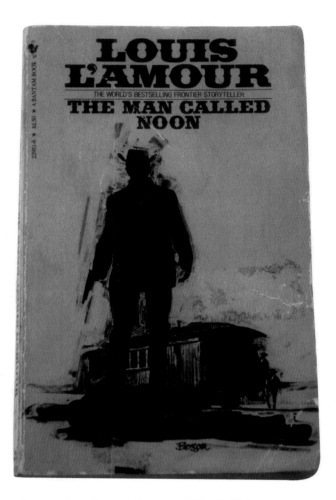

Above: A classic L'Amour's Western, published in 1970.

Returning.

Western writer Loren D. Estleman was also prominent in this decade. He launched his career with *The Oklahoma Punk* in 1976. In the course of his diverse literary career, Estleman invented several famous characters, including Old West Marshall Page Murdoch, and wrote *Bloody Season* in 1987. This was a fictional recreation of the gunfight at the O. K. Corral.

Although Western writing became slightly less mainstream in the 1980s, several distinguished works were published. These included Terry C. Johnson's "Plainsman" novels, which revolve around the action of the Indian Wars. Born in Kansas, Johnston was fascinated by the Old West, and wrote another series based on the Rocky Mountain fur trade era.

Gary Svee is another distinguished writer of Western novels from the 1980's. Born in Billings, Montana, Svee published *Spirit Wolf* in 1987, and his 1990 title, *Sanctuary,* won the Western Writers of America award for the best

Above: Louis L'Amour was known as the "Laureate of the lariat."

Western novel for that year.

The 1990s saw the publication of far fewer Western novels as the genre became less popular. Despite this, several series of Western fiction continued. Perhaps the most famous of these is the "Trailsman" series. Launched in the 1980s, these books were originally written by Jon Sharpe, and are still published under this name by the Penguin Group. Other popular series include the Slocum Westerns, now the longest Western series ever published. These adult-orientated books were written by several authors, all styled after Jake Logan. The most recent title in the series, number 350, *Slocum and the Killers*, was published in March 2008. The Longarm Western series, which also runs to over three hundred volumes, features U.S. Deputy Marshall Curtis Long of Denver, Colorado, and are set in the 1880s. The first book in the series was published in 1978.

The 1990s also saw a new Western writer enter the publishing arena. Don Bendell, who famously fabricated his

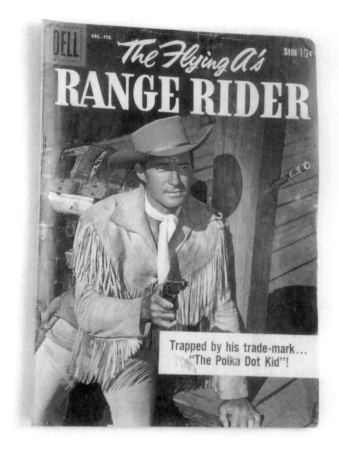

Right and below: Illustrated Western novels from the 1950s.

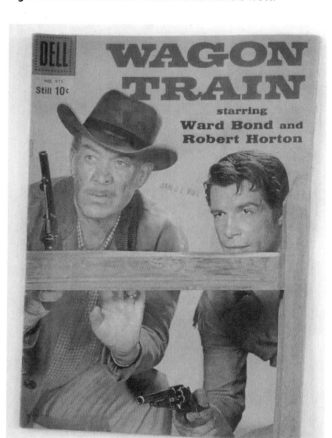

own "Code of the West." Bendell published his first Western novel, *Chief of Scouts* in 1993. He followed this up with *Colt* in 1994, and *War Bonnet* in 2000. Born in 1947, the author describes himself as "an American cowboy."

Western readership steadily declined in the 1990s and 2000s, but many classic Western writers, such as Louis L'Amour, are still very widely read. As a genre, Westerns are still popular, somewhat helped by the ubiquitous movies and television series in this genre.

THE OLD WEST AT THE MOVIES

More than any other medium, the movies have fixed the image of the Old West into millions of minds around the world, and have popularized the legend of the wild frontier. Western movies have also made a massive contribution to the development of the film industry itself, economically and creatively.

Even the earliest Westerns were made with the "formula" that was to define the genre. The frontier is portrayed as the interface between the wilderness and civilization, good and evil, a place where men and women are tested to their limits. Many of Western themes echo the literature that inspired

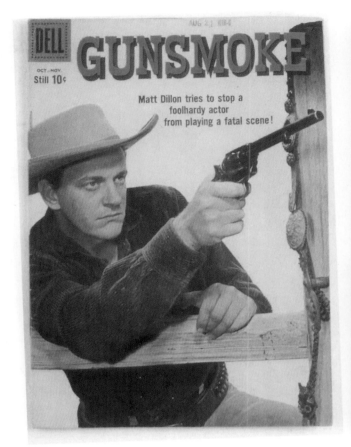

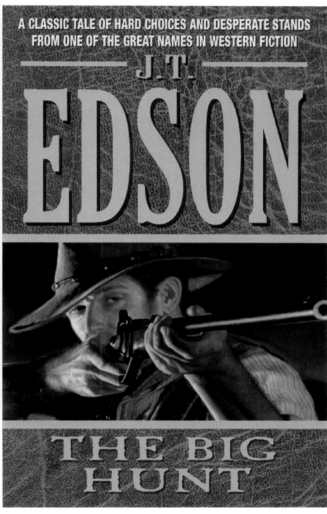

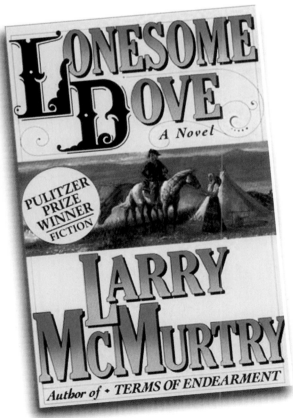

Above: English Western author J.T. Edson never stepped onto American soil.

them, but their visual interpretation of the frontier and the Old West is also fundamental. Some of the first movies ever filmed on location were Westerns, and the sweeping frontier landscape became iconic through these movies, a character in itself. Their specific locations, such as the saloon, the homestead, the fort, the tumbleweed main street, the Native American village also became instantly recognizable. Other elements of these movies, such as their stock cast of characters (cavalrymen, ranchers, cowboys, Indians, lawmen, gunslingers, saloon girls, and good wives) and the Western gear and equipment they catalog (saddles, horse tack, weaponry, blankets, and clothing) are equally familiar.

The unchallenged master of Western location shooting was

John Ford. He was the first director to film a movie in Utah's Monument Valley in his 1939 epic, *Stagecoach*. He went on to use the site in several films, and made its landscape part of the Western iconography.

Western fiction was not the only inspiration behind Western movies. Influences from other art forms also inspired early films, including folk music and painting. The magnificent canvases of Western artist Charles Remington stirred several moviemakers, especially John Ford. The mythology of the West was also important to Western movies: its legendary tales, its colorful characters, and frontier life itself.

The first Westerns were silent movies, and remained so for a couple of decades. The first documented Western film was *Cripple Creek Bar Room Scene*, filmed in 1899. It ran for just one minute. The next was Poker at Dawson City, which also dates from 1899. But *The Great Train Robbery* of 1903 is usually credited as the first "real" Western. This one-reel film was directed by Edwin S. Porter, and ran for twelve minutes. The film also launched the career of the first on-screen cowboy, Bronco Billy Anderson. Anderson continued to make Western films until *Son of A Gun* in 1919. In 1905, *The Great Train Robbery* became the main attraction at the first nickelodeon. Two other notable Westerns were also released in 1903, *Kit Carson* and *The Pioneers*. *A California Hold Up* (1906) was the first Western to be filmed entirely on location.

Westerns soon started to feature the cream of contemporary acting talent. Mary Pickford starred in the *Twisted Trail* (1910), while Lillian Gish and Mae Marsh appeared in 1915's *Birth of a Nation*. Western movies also began to feature real life characters, such as Wyatt Earp in *The Half Breed* (1919), and Buffalo Bill Cody in the eponymous *Adventures of Buffalo Bill Cody,* released in 1917. This trend continues today.

Silent-era Westerns soon began to make their own stars. Ex-Shakespearian actor William S. Hart starred in many Western films between 1915 and 1925, including *The Narrow Trail* (1917). Hart's film character was often accompanied by his famous mount, Fritz. Other stars from this time included Tom Mix, who starred in several major Westerns, including *Riders of the Purple Sage* in 1925, and Harry Carey, who appeared as frontiersman Cheyenne Harry in several John Ford movies. Other distinguished film actors of this time included Hoot Gibson, Buck Jones, Tim Holt, Bill Elliott, and Johnny Mack Brown.

In the 1920s, Western films were often rated as B-movies, but director James Cruze took the genre up a gear with the first large-scale Western epic, 1923's *The Covered Wagon*. Production of the movie cost Paramount the enormous sum of $800,000, but it recouped over $4 million at the box office. By the end of the 1920s, the era of the silent Western was ending. Director Victor Schertinger made one of the last, 1929's *Redskin*. The first sound Western made by a major studio was released in the same year. In Old Arizona came from Fox-Movietone, and starred Warner Baxter.

The movie that is considered by many to be the first modern Western, *The Virginian*, was also launched in 1929. Directed by Victor Fleming and starring Gary Cooper, the film was the third screen version of Owen Wister's classic Western novel.

Several influential directors who had cut their artistic teeth on silent Westerns went on to achieve even greater success in the talkies. These men included John Ford, John Huston, Howard Hawks, and Cecil B. De Mille. The decades of the 1930s, 1940s, and 1950s are often considered the "Golden Era" of Western movies. Many great stars, film techniques, and directors certainly owe their fame to Western movies of this period.

John Ford made a smooth transition into talking Westerns, and made fifteen major films in this genre. His 1939 film *Stage Coach* is important for many artistic reasons, but it is best remembered as the movie that projected John Wayne from B-Westerns to stardom. The pair went on to make several classic films in the Western genre, including *Fort Apache* (1948), *She Wore a Yellow Ribbon* (1949), *The Searchers* (1956), and *The Man Who Shot Liberty Valance* (1962). The Western genre made Wayne's career, and he became the most popular and durable of all of its stars. His career spanned several decades. Two of his memorable later works are *True Grit* (1969) and *The Shootist* (1976).

John Ford's Westerns launched several other high profile stars. Henry Fonda starred in the 1939 film *Drums Along the Mohawk* alongside Claudette Colbert, and in 1946's *My Darling Clementine* with Victor Mature.

Errol Flynn was another Hollywood star whose career included a stint making Westerns. His first, *Dodge City* (1939), was an early Technicolor movie in which he co-starred with Olivia de Havilland. Flynn also starred in *Virginia* and *Sante Fe Trail*, which were both released in 1940, and in the 1941 film *They Died With Their Boots On*. Ronald Reagan co-starred in the latter.

Howard Hawks, noted for his versatility as a director, also

made several successful Westerns during the genre's Golden Age. His 1948 *Red River* stars John Wayne, and tells the story of the first cattle drive along the Chisholm Trail, fictionalized by writer Borden Chase. The United States Library of Congress rates the film as "culturally significant." Chase also wrote screenplays for *Bend of the River* (1952), and *The Far Country* (1954). Hawks directed several other Westerns, including *Rio Bravo* in 1959. This film starred the somewhat unlikely pairing of John Wayne and Dean Martin.

Known for his lavish epics, Cecil B. De Mille brought his special directing talents to the Western with his 1937 film, *The Plainsman*. Starring Gary Cooper, the film features a complete restaging of the Battle of Little Big Horn, shot entirely on location in Montana.

King Vidor, who is credited with the longest ever career in movie directing, also made a few Westerns during this period. These included *The Texas Rangers* (1936) and *Duel in the Sun*, launched in 1946. This film was produced by David O. Selznick, and, because of its many love scenes, became colloquially known as "Lust in the Dust."

The first ever color Western, *Billy the Kid,* was released in 1941. The movie was David Miller's remake of the black-and-white 1930 film of the same name.

The 1930s were the heyday of a Western subgenre, the singing cowboy movie. Gene Autry debuted in *Old Sante Fe* in 1934, and went on to make over a hundred films in his long and successful career. Autry made the "singing cowboy" genre hugely popular, and several other actors made movies of this type, including Bing Crosby (*Rhythm on the Range*, 1936), Tex Ritter, Bob Baker, and William "Hopalong Cassidy" Boyd. Gene Autry became heavily identified with his on-screen persona, and conceived his own "Cowboy Code." His basic credo was that a cowboy never shoots first, never takes unfair advantage, tells the truth, helps people in distress, and is always a patriot. Autry's clean-cut image suited the times, and propelled him to enormous popularity.

In the 1940s, Roy Rogers succeeded Gene Autry as the singing "King of Cowboys." He had played Autry's sidekick, Frog Millhouse, in many movies, but took his first lead in *Under Western Stars*. Rogers also went on to have a long and distinguished career on screen and television, and was one of the first stars to inspire a marketing phenomenon. He endorsed many products, including cowboy dolls, novels, and a comic strip.

By complete contrast, several "Noir" Westerns were also released in this decade, including the famous *Pursued* (1947).

Above: John Ford (right) made a smooth transition into directing talking Westerns, and made fifteen major films in this genre.

Above: John Ford's Western movies launched several high profile careers, including that of John Wayne, seen here with his mentor.

Left: A still from *The Great Train Robbery* of 1903.

Right: Tom Mix was an early Western star.

You don't think I want to do this Molly? But you won't ask me to run away—

THE Virginian

WITH
GARY COOPER
AND
WALTER HUSTON
RICHARD ARLEN
AND MARY BRIAN
A VICTOR FLEMING
PRODUCTION

a Paramount Picture

Above: The Virginian was launched in 1929. It starred Gary Cooper.

Opposite: A poster for John Wayne's 1935 film, *The New Frontier*.

Raoul Walsh directed this tense psychological drama. Shot in black and white, it starred Robert Mitchum. This Austrian-American director also contributed several artistic films to the Western genre, including two Technicolor films, *The Return of Frank James* (starring Henry Fonda) in 1940, and *Western Union* (based on the Zane Grey novel) in 1941. Walsh's 1952 film, *Rancho Notorious* starred Marlene Dietrich, bizarrely cast as a criminal matriarch.

The Western genre continued to develop in the 1950s, both artistically and technically. Widescreen Westerns now became the norm. Cinema Scope was introduced in 1953 and Vista Vision in 1954. These formats did particular justice to the expansive frontier landscape and became closely identified with epic Westerns. Perhaps the epitome of this sub genre is *The Big Country*, William Wyler's big budget picture of 1958. Other upbeat movies in this style include Howard Hawk's *The Big Sky* (1952), John Farrow's *Honcho* (1953), and *The Alamo* (1960), directed by John Wayne.

The Noir Western also retained its popularity in this decade. Anthony Mann directed several films in this style, which were also notable for their wonderful evocations of the

Previous pages:
John Wayne in two
Western classics, *Rio
Lobo* and *The
Cowboys.*

Right: Errol Flynn's
career included several
memorable Westerns.

frontier landscape. Most of Mann's Westerns starred James Stewart, including 1952's iconic *Bend of the River* and 1955's *The Far Country.* Mann also worked with Henry Fonda, Anthony Perkins, and Gary Cooper. His collaboration with the director greatly enhanced Stewart's career, and he had become Hollywood's top male star by the end of the decade.

Budd Boetticher was another notable director of the 1950s. His films included *Seven Men From Now* (1956), starring Lee Marvin, and *Ride Lonesome* (1959), starring Randolph Scott. This movie also introduced James Coburn to the public.

Several strands of new thinking also influenced Western films of this period. 1953's *Shane* was director George Stevens's accurate portrayal of pioneer life, starring Alan Ladd as a classic Western hero, while director Delmer Daves's 1950 film *Broken Arrow* was the first Western to show any real understanding of Native Americans. Daves went on to make *Pony Express* and *Arrowhead* (both released in 1953).

Perhaps the apex of all Western movie making was achieved in this decade in director Fred Zinnemann's only Western, *High Noon.* Many critics believe that this is not only the most important movie of the 1950s, but also the best Western ever made. Starring Gary Cooper and Grace Kelly, this 1952 movie was based on a pulp magazine short story, "The Tin Star." Cooper plays Will Kane, a beleaguered town marshal who must tackle a gang of killers by himself. Although Zinnemann made the film with a limited budget of $750,000, and at lightening speed in only thirty-two days, *High Noon* has became a perennial classic. It is also the movie most requested for viewing by American presidents.

Although the popularity of 1950s Western television series somewhat dented the supremacy of the big screen Western, the 1960s saw a revival in their popularity. The style of Western movies also underwent a substantial change in the 1960s. "Revisionist" Westerns saw a harder and more critical approach to the subject matter, and their heroes tended to be more bitter, vengeful, and violent. Cue Clint Eastwood.

Eastwood began his Western career playing Rowdy Yates in the long-running television series *Rawhide,* but his appearance in several excellent movies ultimately earned him John Wayne's mantle as the leading man of Westerns. Although Eastwood had worked in several low quality Western movies, his fame was greatly enhanced by his starring roles in Sergio Leone's Spaghetti Westerns. He starred as the charismatic "Man with No Name" in Leone's monumental trilogy, *A Fistful of Dollars, For a Few Dollars More,* and *The Good, the Bad, and the Ugly.* The heroes of these films were far grittier, more complex, and less noble than those of earlier Westerns. Indeed, they often had a dark, sadistic streak. Leone also redefined the look of "cowboy" characters as ragged and dusty rather than pristine and salubrious. He also used Ennio Morricone's atmospheric music to intensify the electric atmosphere of his moody cinematic technique. Although Leone made his early films in Italy and Spain to save money, his later work, such as *Once Upon a Time in America* (Paramount, 1967), was filmed in the West. Leone also used seasoned Western stars, such as Henry Fonda, James Coburn, Charles Bronson, and Lee Van Cleef in his films.

The Magnificent Seven was another notable film from this period. Released in 1960, it was directed by John Sturges, "the dean of big-budget action movies" who had also made *Gunfight at the OK Corral* in 1957. The movie starred Yul Brynner, Charles Bronson, and Steve McQueen (among others) as a group of gunmen hired to protect a Mexican village. Although the film had the usual frontier themes, it was actually based on Japanese director Akira Kurosawa's 1954 film, *The Seven Samurai.* Another pivotal 1960's film was Sam Peckinpah's *The Wild Bunch.* Although the movie starred a number of Western veterans, including William Holden and Ernest Borgnine, it heralded a new style of movie making, notable for its extreme violence and technical dexterity.

Several movies parodying traditional Western themes were also released in the 1960s. Lee Marvin and Jane Fonda starred in the 1965 film *Cat Ballou,* while James Garner appeared in 1969's *Support Your Local Sheriff,* directed by Burt Kennedy. Mel Brookes followed this vein of comedy in his 1974 film *Blazing Saddles,* which starred the mad-eyed Gene Wilder.

Left: Dean Martin plays the drunken gunfighter in 1970's *Rio Bravo.*

Below: Gene Autry began his career as "Oklahoma's Yodeling Cowboy."

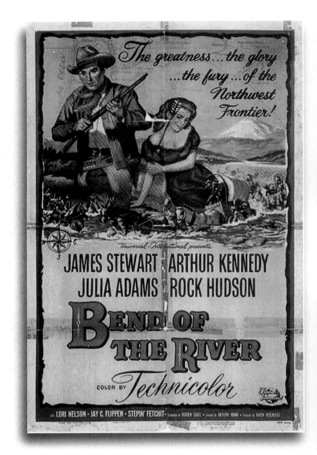

Above and left: Jimmy Stewart made several Westerns including 1952's Bend of the River.

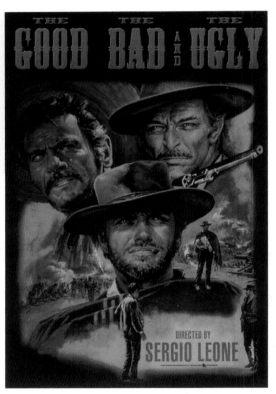

Above: A poster for the classic Sergio Leone Western *The Good, the Bad and the Ugly*, starring Clint Eastwood.

The 1970s was a difficult decade for Western films. Not only were fewer serious films made in the genre, but some of the great Western practitioners also died, including John Wayne and John Ford. The pair had released their final film, *Rio Lobo*, in 1970. Despite his encroaching illness, Wayne released fourteen new films in the 1970s, including several classics such as *Chisum* and *The Cowboys*.

The decline of Westerns was even more marked in the 1980s. Old Western movies were now shown in "dead" television slots, effectively devaluing the genre. Their morality seemed flawed by modern standards, especially their unsympathetic portrayal of Native Americans. Several Westerns that were released, including Michael Cimino's *Heaven's Gate* (1980), were complete flops at the box office. This film was so financially disastrous that it contributed to the demise of United Artists.

By contrast, the 1990s saw an upturn in the fortunes of the Western. There was a great upsurge in interest in the real, historical characters of the frontier, and many Westerns were made around this extraordinary coterie. These movies included 1993's *Tombstone* (about Wyatt Earp and Doc Holliday), 1994's *Wyatt Earp*, and 1995's *Wild Bill* (Hickok, of

course). A new generation of stars was also cast in Western roles, including Kevin Costner, Kurt Russell, and Jeff Bridges. More "traditional" Western themes were still explored in contemporary movies, but with a new twist.

Clint Eastwood's 1992 film, *Unforgiven*, explodes many

Above: Gary Cooper in the Western classic, *High Noon*. A movie that many believe to be the finest Western ever made.

Above: 1960's *The Magnificent Seven*, starring
Yul Brynner and Steve McQueen.

Right: Clint Eastwood starred as Rowdy Yates in
1950's television series, *Rawhide.*

myths of the Old West. In this film, the frontier is violent, and its men morally ambiguous. The easy certainties of early Westerns have gone forever. Eastwood made the film as a tribute to Sergio Leone's Spaghetti Westerns. It was a great critical success: only the third ever Western to win the Academy Award for Best Picture. It also grossed over $100 million.

Kevin Costner's *Dances with Wolves* (1990) was equally subversive to the usual Western clichés. Not only is the movie very sympathetic in its treatment of the Sioux and their way of life, but it also demonstrates the huge cultural differences between Native American tribes. The film won seven Academy Awards, and a Golden Globe. This style of "revisionist" film had originated in the 1950s with pieces such as *The Last Wagon* (1956), but Costner's movie was the culmination of this Western subgenre.

The revival of interest in Westerns continued into the 2000s. Although contemporary Westerns are often set in the classic frontier landscape, and have many elements of the genre (lawmen, gunmen, saloons, and ranches), these movies also explore less conventional subjects. Robert Rodriguez's *Once Upon A Time in Mexico*, for example, explores Mexico's drug underworld. Although the move is set in the present day, it deals with classic Western material, violence, revenge, and murdered families. Controversially, Ang Lee's 2005 movie *Brokeback Mountain* deals with a romantic homosexual relationship between two latter-day cowboys. The film was hugely successful, and is ranked as the eighth highest-grossing romantic film ever made. Wim Wender's film from the same year, *Don't Come Knocking* is his comedy tribute to Western stars. In a highly unusual twist on the genre, the movie both uses and parodies many Western clichés.

2007's *The Assassination of Jesse James by the Coward Robert Ford* is a more straightforward Western, with many of the classic elements: loneliness, the omnipresent frontier landscape, and casual violence. Based on Rob Hansen's 1983 novel, it also portrays a Western legend. Most critics rated the film highly, particularly the central performances from Brad Pitt and Casey Affleck.

THE OLD WEST ON TELEVISION

A fiery horse with the speed of light, a cloud of dust, even a hearty "Hi-ho Silver!" The Lone Ranger!

Western series date back to the very early days of television, the direct descendants of the radio Westerns of early decades.

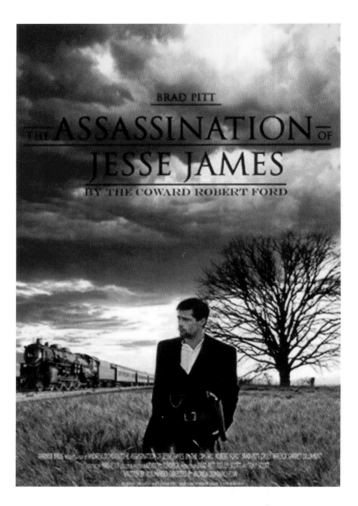

Above: 2007 saw the launch of *The Assassination of Jesse James by the Coward Robert Ford.*

Radio Westerns often featured the so-called "singing cowboys," Gene Autry, Roy Rogers, Rex Allen and cowgirl Dale Evans. The popularity of television Westerns peaked in 1959, when there were no fewer than twenty-six prime time Western shows. Although their popularity has gone through peaks and troughs since then, the Western format has proved to be highly adaptable, and has survived to the present.

The very first television Western, Hopalong Cassidy, was first aired on June 24, 1949. Based on Clarence E. Mulford's cowboy character, the original shows were re-edited B-movies. But these were so successful that NBC commissioned some original half hour episodes. The show rated seventh in the 1949 Nielsen ratings. A radio version of the show was also launched.

By contrast, *The Lone Ranger* show began as a radio

Above: *The Lone Ranger* starring Clayton Moore.

Right: Roy Rogers with his wife Dale Evans. The couple was married for 51 years.

Western for WXYZ in Detroit. It was first broadcast in 1933 and ran for 2,956 episodes. ABC launched a television version of this highly successful formula in 1949, with Clayton Moore in the eponymous role. The series survived until 1957.

The Roy Rogers Show was another early television Western that ran for a hundred episodes between 1951 and 1957. This NBC show also starred Roger's wife, Dale Evans. Another iconic Western dating from this early television era was Gunsmoke. This show had also originated on radio, first airing in 1952. The television version was launched in 1955. This story of Marshall Matt Dillon became the longest running prime time drama in American television history, surviving until 1975. James Arness remained in the lead role for virtually every episode.

NBC's *Bonanza* was also long-lived, surviving for fourteen years. It became the network's second longest running drama series, and the first hour-long serial to be shot in color. It aired between 1959 and 1973, and starred Pernell Roberts and Lorne Green. CBS launched the rival Western series *Rawhide* in 1959. The program is now most famous for launching Clint Eastwood's career in the role of Rowdy Yates ("the idiot of the plains," as the star described his former role). Another show that launched an illustrious career was ABC's *Maverick*, a Western series with a comedy twist. It starred James Garner as Bret Maverick until 1960, an adventurous gambler roaming the Old West in search of a poker game. The show aired between 1957 and 1962.

The 1960s saw a continuation of the Western genre on television. NBC's *The Virginian* ran for 249 episodes between 1962 and 1967. It starred James Drury and Doug McClure. As this was cancelled, NBC launched *The High Chapparal*, which survived until 1971. The series was set in the 1870's, and featured Leif Erickson as Big John Cannon.

Although the 1970s and 1980s saw the launch of several new television Westerns, they were not necessarily set in the

Right: *Gunsmoke* was an iconic television Western of the 1950s, and starred James Arness as Marshal Matt Dillon.

Old West, or infused with the genre's traditional themes. These new series included several extremely successful vehicles, *McCloud, Little House on the Prairie*, and *The Life and Times of Grizzly Adams*. *McCloud* starred Dennis Weaver as Marshal Sam McCloud, a lawman from New Mexico, seconded to the New York City Police Department.

Little House on the Prairie was based on Laura Ingalls Wilder's 1935 book, which was inspired by her Midwestern childhood. This important NBC series, set in Walnut Grove, Minnesota, aired between 1974 and 1983. *Grizzly Adams* was also loosely based on real-life characters, in this case, the famous trapper John Capen "Grizzly" Adams. The series was derived from an extremely successful 1974 movie and ran from 1977 to 1978. It gained a thirty-two per cent market share and capitalized on interest in the growing ecology movement.

The 1990s saw the launch of a two extremely successful

Western series. CBS's gritty *Lonesome Dove* starred Robert Duvall, and was made with highly authentic production values. The network also made the long-running and successful *Dr. Quinn, Medicine Woman*, which ran for one hundred and fifty episodes. Starring the English actress Jane Seymour, the multi-Emmy Award winning series ran for six seasons between 1993 and 1998, and aired in a hundred countries. With a timeline beginning in 1867, the series is set in the town of Colorado Springs. Although the program had a strong atmosphere of the Old West, it dealt with new themes and had a completely original set of characters.

1990s also saw the release of a number of made-for-television Western movies. These included *Conagher* (1991), and *Shaughnessy* (1996), both based on Louis L'Amour novels. This well-known Western writer had also contributed an episode to *Maverick* and wrote a seventeen-episode television miniseries, based on his book *Hondo*.

The television Westerns of the 2000s have followed the trend of their big screen counterparts, with their action based on real-life characters. HBO's Deadwood featured many historical Westerners, including Wild Bill Hickok, Calamity Jane, and Wyatt Earp. The drama ran for three seasons between 2004 and 2006.

In all its different forms, the Western has not only been a foundation of American popular culture, but has also played a huge part in shaping it. Starting in the written form, and

Above: Dan Blockner, Lorne Greene, and Michael Landon starred in *Bonanza*.

Right: The cast of *The High Chaparral*, with Leif Erickson in the center.

evolving into movies, radio, and television, Westerns have been the backbone of American entertainment for nearly two centuries. The formats and revenue generated by the Western genre have influenced a huge swathe of popular culture, and continue to do so. Westerns have not only revealed a fascinating aspect of American culture and history to an enthralled world, but have also helped to remind us of the origins of America life itself.

Right: James Garner as Bret Maverick in ABC's *Maverick*.

WESTERN TOYS

The many Western television series of the 1950s engendered a huge marketing phenomenon. A plethora of products were launched with a Western theme, however tenuous. These included "Wild West" versions of many existing products, such as handkerchiefs, pockets knives, ballpoint pens, toothpicks, lunchboxes, and cups. The enormous popularity of Western toys and outfits also dates from this time, and continues today. Many of the most successful toys were tied-in to specific Western television series, and endorsed by the most famous characters: Roy Rogers, Maverick, and Davy Crocket.

Right: In the 1950s, every little boy wanted to be a cowboy.

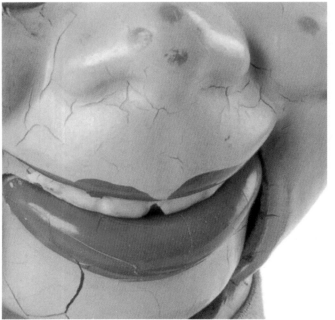

Above: *The Howdy Doody Show* began in 1947 featuring the cowboy marionette. Howdy Doody lived in Doodyville, an imaginary Western town.

Children longed to dress in cowboy outfits, just like their heroes, and a great variety of these were sold, complete with boots, vests, chaps, jackets, and Stetsons. Cowboy pistols, rifles, holsters, and gun belts were also hugely popular, and offered by a wide variety of toy manufacturers. Children also dressed as lawmen and Native Americans, with star badges and feather headdresses.

The Marx toy company was one of the most important manufacturers of the period, and launched many different Western toys. Louis Marx realized the huge potential of the mania for Westerns. They bought several licenses to make toys tied-in with television series, including the Roy Rogers Ranch and the Lone Ranger play set. But Marx soon realized that these licenses were very expensive, and began to manufacture generic toys based on classic Western legends and characters, such as Wyatt Earp, General Custer, Chief Cherokee, Sheriff Garrett, and Daniel Boone, the Wilderness Scout. Some of their toys became classics of the genre, including the Fort Apache Stockade and Rin Tin Tin Fort Apache. Their Jamie and Jane West Western figures stayed in production for several decades, together with a great range of mounts and accessories. Marx also made a plethora of Indian drums, Western costumes, colts and buffalo, and fort accessories. The success of its Western toys was one factor that propelled Marx to huge success. The company's founder, Louis Marx, became known as "The Toy King," and "The Henry Ford of the Toy Industry."

The Stuart Manufacturing Company also manufactured Western figures between 1953 and 1969. These included the Roy Rogers ranch set, complete with plastic horses. Milton Bradley marketed the Buckaroo Game, which featured a backing plastic mule, which had to be carefully loaded with "a whole mess of gear… for a trip to the gold mines." Toy manufacturer Yankiboy made Indian squaw costumes, and an Indian Tee Pee, while Nylint offered a successful Howdy Doody doll.

Several manufacturers made toy cap guns, and of these, Hubley was the most famous and successful. Several of the models they manufactured between 1920 and 1965 became iconic, especially their Texan and Cowboy cap guns. The company was based in Lancaster, Pennsylvania. Hubley also made Colt 45's, Miniature 44's, Frontier Rifles, and Dagger Derringers. Other cap manufacturers included Daisy, Wyandotte, Actoy, Kenton, Buzz Henry, Lone Star, and Marx.

Modern versions of most classic Western toys are still available today, but there are also modern twists on the theme. The 1995 movie *Toy Story* launched a new version of the cowboy doll, based on the movie's main character, Sheriff Woody. In the film, Woody was a product inspired by a fictional 1950s television series, *Woody's Roundup*. Woody is the brave and resourceful leader of the movie's toys, and is joined by cowgirl doll Jesse in the 1999 sequel.

These two pairs of children's cowboy boots were made in the 1940s and 1950s. One pair is ornately stitched, and has exaggerated pointed toes. The other pair is made in the roper style, from plain black cowhide, with rounded toes and heels.

The King of the Cowboys

The Roy Rogers jacket was part of the marketing phenomenon that surrounded this classic television Western. "The King of the Cowboys" inspired this beautiful buckskin fringed jacket. The label also features his trusty steed, Trigger. The jacket was undoubtedly very precious to its original owner, "Mike."

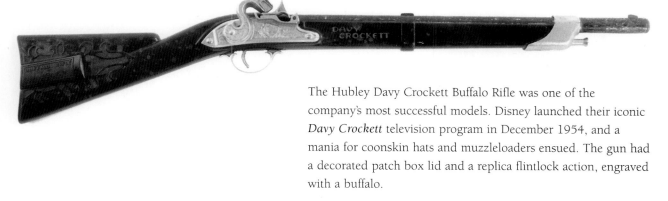

The Hubley Davy Crockett Buffalo Rifle was one of the company's most successful models. Disney launched their iconic *Davy Crockett* television program in December 1954, and a mania for coonskin hats and muzzleloaders ensued. The gun had a decorated patch box lid and a replica flintlock action, engraved with a buffalo.

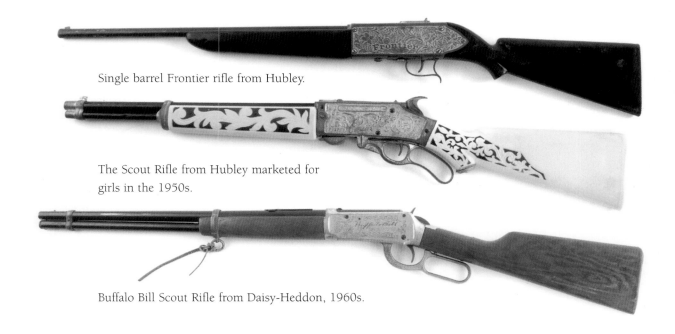

Single barrel Frontier rifle from Hubley.

The Scout Rifle from Hubley marketed for girls in the 1950s.

Buffalo Bill Scout Rifle from Daisy-Heddon, 1960s.

The Rifleman

Hubley bought the contract to produce the famous "Rifleman" gun based on the Chuck Connors television show. The series first aired in 1958.

Daisy's Red Ryder air rifles were more generic guns. The company had manufactured air rifles since the 1880's, but branded their guns with Frontier imagery in the 1950's to capitalize on the fascination with everything Western.

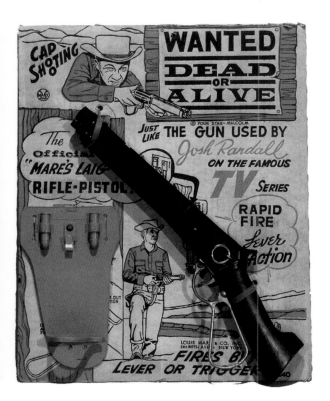

Marx and Esquire made these two versions of bounty hunter Josh Randall's gun. The toy weapons were part of the merchandising package surrounding the Wanted Dead or Alive television series. Starring Steve McQueen as the bounty-hunting cowboy, the series first aired in 1958. Marx claimed that their gun was the official toy version of the sawn off and holstered "Mare's Laig" rifle.

These Kenton cap pistols date from the 1920s, andtheir clumsy firing hammers fired simple caps. The company's products became more sophisticated as Western-inspired audiences became more sophisticated.

This Hubley twin holster set dates from the 1950s and was one of the most popular toy caps guns from this time. The holsters and belt buckle are decorated with classic Western imagery; steers' heads, wagon train, H-rivets, and Western stars. The pistols fired reel caps.

The Maverick Pistol was television tie-in product, made by Esquire Novelty/Leslie-Henry. The ABC series, "sponsored by Kaiser Aluminum" starred James Garner. The gun is a bronze long-hammer revolving cylinder pistol, with white stag horn grips and a fancy leather holster.

These toy Derringers reflected the more sophisticated Western television series of the 1960s, where a new breed of television hero carried concealed weapons. The Nichols versions fire dummy bullets. Marx also copied this system. The unusual Mattel concealed "Buckle Gun" pops out for use!

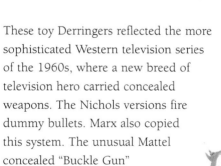

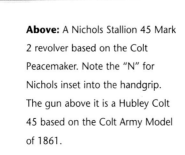

Above: A Nichols Stallion 45 Mark 2 revolver based on the Colt Peacemaker. Note the "N" for Nichols inset into the handgrip. The gun above it is a Hubley Colt 45 based on the Colt Army Model of 1861.

Mattel made the popular Fanner range in the 1960s. The Shootin' Shell Fanner shot "Greenie" cartridges, just like the real thing! More conventionally, the Fanner 50 used conventional caps.

Hubley's generic toys included their Western and Texan lines. The Westerns were made with a choice of four handgrip colors, and were decorated with steer's heads. They fired roll caps. The Hubley Texans date from the 1950s and were made in three different finishes, silver, gold, and pewter.

The 1950s cap gun craze led to an explosion in different firing systems. Some of these were quite sophisticated. These included Mammoth's "Guaranteed Sure Fire" caps, Kilgore's "Bang Caps," and Halco "Jet" roll caps.

This selection of Western accessories includes Marshal and Sheriff badges, handcuffs, and jangling spurs. They all date from the 1950s and 1960s.

The Unique Art Manufacturing Company of Newark made the "Rodeo Joe Crazy Car." It is perfectly in tune with the 1950s fascination with everything Western. This wind-up tin toy featured detailed graphics and Western styling themes, such as "leather" stitching, rope work lettering, and bucking bronco motif.

The Haji Mansei Toy Company of Tokyo, Japan made the "Horse and Western Rider" tin litho toy in 1951. They specialized in making tin tanks, and the toy was their attempt to cash in on the 1950s mania for everything Western.

Woody is a new generation toy inspired by the West, manufactured to tie-in with the 1995 film Toy Story. The doll is based on the film's starring character, and says several lines from the movie when his middle shirt button is pressed, including "Wanna go to a round up?" and "Glad to see you Deputy." Thinkway Thinking Toys made Woody in China.

INDEX

Figures in **bold** refer to illustrations.

A

Abilene **10**, 113, 149, 151, 188
Actoy 241
Adair, John G. 19
Adams, Andy 215
Adams, John Capen "Grizzly" 236
Affleck, Casey 234
Ahfitche, Governor **54**
Alhambra Saloon and Gambling Hall 147
Allen, Rex 234
Allison, Robert Clay 98, 103, **104**
Ames 68
Anderson, Bronco Billy 222
angora chaps 22
Antrim, Harry McCarthy 107, 108
Apache 49, 70
Apache Scouts **49**
Apache Wars 72
Appomattox 65
Arapaho 17, 184
Argonauts 150
Arikara War 47
Arkansas City, Kansas 207
Arkansas River 82, 95
Arness, James 235
The Assassination of Jesse James by the Coward Robert Ford 234
Ashley, William 134
Ashley-Henry Expedition 134
Asiatic cholera 152
The Authentic Life of Billy the Kid 112
Autry, Gene 223, 229, 234

B

Bader and Laubner's Saloon **159**
Baker, Bob 223
Bandana **21**
Baptists 138
barbed wire **18**
Battle of Brandy Station 65

Battle of Gaines' Mill 72
Battle of Little Big Horn 52, 67, **69**
Battle of Slim Buttes 72
Battle of Washita River 67
Bear River City, Wyoming **179**
Beckwourth, Jim **134**
Bell, J. W. 109
Bellafonte, Harry 140
Ballard, Willis Todhunter 217
Bend of the River 230
Bendell, Don 220
"Big Nose" Kate 103, 149, 166, **167**
The Big Sky 218
Billy the Kid **108**, 109
black gold 211
Black Hawk **47**
Black Kettle 67
Blackburn, Tom W. 216
Blevins, Andy 99
Blevins, John 99
Blevins, Sam 99
Blockner, Dan 236
The Blue and the Gray 95
Blue Duck **94**
Boetticher, Budd 228
Bonanza **236**
Bonney, William H. 109
Boomer's Camp 207
Boomers, Sooners, and Moonshiners 204-211
Boone, Daniel 240
Bowles, Samuel 180
Boyd, William (Hopalong Cassidy) 223
Brand, Max 216
Bret Maverick 237
Brannan, Samuel 154
Bridger, Jim 134
Bridges, Jeff 230
Broadwell, Dick 111
Brocious, "Curley Bill" 101
Bronco Bill Charlie 142
Bronson, Charles 228
Brookes, Mel 228
Brothels 162
Brown, Neal 101
Brown's Hole 188
Bryant, Blackfaced Charlie 112

Brynner, Yul 228, 232
Buck and the Preacher 140
Buckaroos 10
Buckaroo game 241
buffalo **18**, 184
buffalo chaps **22**
Buffalo Bill 20, **53**, 63, 67, 142, 165, 184, 215, 222
Buffalo Bill's Wild West Show **28**, **29**, 56
Buffalo Nickel 57
Buffalo Soldiers **72**, **73**
Buffalo Steaks with Chipotle-Coffee Rub 41
Buffalo skin gloves **78**
Bulette, Julia 162
Bull Run 62
Bullion, Laura **167**
Burnside carbine **63**
Bush, Corporal Frederich **63**
butternut **75**
branding irons **28**
bunkhouse **20**
Buzz Henry 241

C

Cairns, Jimmy 100
Calamity Jane 20, **165**, 236
Caldwell, Kansas **16**
California Gold Rush 146
California Trail 150
Callaway, George Dickerson Sr. **15**
Callaway, William Theodore 15
canned food **32**
Cannon, Big John 235
carbine boot **69**
Carey, Harry 222
Carlyle, deputy James 109
Carpenter, Helen 170
Carson, Kit 135, 215
Cartwright, Peter 139
Cattle Kate 166
cavalry hat **77**
cavalry saber **68**
caviada/caballa 23
Central Pacific Railroad 178, 181, 185
chalans 13

Chancellorsville 65
Chaplin, Charlie 154
chaps 22
charros 13
Chase, Borden 223
Cherokee 47, 50
Cherokee Bill 91, **93**
Cheyenne 17, 70, 184
Chickasaw 24
Chisholm, Jesse 14
Chisholm Trail 14, **15**, 17, 223
Christie, Ned 87
Chuck Wagon 30-43, **32**, **33**, **35**
Chuck Wagon Beans 39
Chuck Wagon Coffee 37
Chuck Wagon Stew **41**
Cimino, Michael 230
Civil War 13, 14, 179
Claims Office, Round Pond **204**
Clark, Dick 147
Clark, Walter Vantilburg 216
Coburn, James 228
Cody, William F., q.v. Buffalo Bill
Coe, Charlie 147
Coe, Phil 113
Coffeyville, Kansas 110, 111
Colbert, Chunk 104
Colbert, Claudette 222
Colt Buntline Special 100
Colt Frontier 88
Colt Peacemaker 247
Colt pistols **63**
Colt revolvers 116-117
Colt .45 revolver **67**
Colt's Competitors 118-119
Columbus, Christopher 46
Comanche 50, 68, 70
Condon Bank **110**
Confederate cavalry officer's coat 75
Connors, Chuck 244
Cook, Captain **78**
Cooke, General Philip St. George 62
"cookie" **33**
Cooper, Andy 99, 100
Cooper, Gary 222, 223, 228,

231
Cooper, James Fennimore 212
Cora, Charles 145
Corinne, Utah 180, **181**
Costner, Kevin 230, 234
Council Bluffs 178
Cowboy Beans 39
The Cowboys 228
cow cavalry 12
cowboys 8-29
cowboy boots **21**
Cowboy Sausage Sweet Taters 37
cowgirl **164**
Cowgirl Hall of Fame 165
Cozad, Nebraska **180**
cracker cowboy 12
Crapper Jack's Dance Hall **160**
Crazy horse 52, 68
Creek 50
Cribs 162
Crittenden, Governor Thomas 106
Crocket, Davy 238, 243
Crosby, Bing 223
Cruz, Florentino 101
Cruze, James 222
Cumberland Presbyterians 138
Currier and Ives 144, 178
Curry, Kid 166
Custer, Boston 67
Custer, Elizabeth Bacon 67, 184
Custer, General George Armstrong **69**, 78, **79**, 240
Custer, Captain Thomas 67, 78
Custer's 7th Cavalry **64**, 67, 78
Custer's Last Stand **66**

D
Daisy 241, 244
Dakota Territory 168
Dalton, Bob 111
Dalton, Brat 111
Dalton, Frank 91
Dalton Gang 111, 167
Dalton, Gratton 112
Dance rattle 56
"daughters of sin" 162
Davies, Anna 91
Davies, Senator Henry 91
Davies, Marion 139
Daves, Delmer 228
Davis, Maud 166
David, Miriam 170
Day, Peter 178
De Ville, Cecil B. 222, 223

Deadwood 113, 147, 148, 168
"Dead Man's Hand" 113, 148
Deano, Lottie 148, 160
Deringers and Vest Guns 130-131
Devol, George 146
DeVoto, Bernard 19
Diamond Toothed Gerty 160
Dietrich, Marlene 224
Disney 243
Dobie, J. Frank 216
"Doc" Durrant **179**
Dodge City **96**, 102, **103**
Dodge City Gang 150
Dodge City Peace Commission 99, 101, 103
"doves of the roost" 162
Dodge, General Grenville Mellen 184
Dragoons (1st and 2nd) 63
dreaming sack 23
Drury, James 235
Duffield, Frank 168
Duniway, Abigail Scott 156
Dutch oven **40**
Duvall, Robert 236

E
Edson, J. T. (John Thomas) 218, 221
El Dorado Gambling Saloon 146
El Paso Hotel 29
Ellsworth, Kansas 14, 192
Ellsworth, Reverend W.I. 139
Elmer, Oscar 140
enamelware **37**
Earp, Bessie 167
Earp, Morgan 100
Earp, Virgil 100
Earp, Wyatt 100, 103, 147, 189, 222, 230, 236, 240
Eastwood, Clint 140, 228, 230, 232, 235
Elephant Saloon 148
Erikson, Leif 235, 236
Esquire Novelty 245, 246
Estleman, Loren D. 219
Evans, Dale 234, 235

F
"fair belles" 162
"fallen angels" 162
"fallen frails" 162
Fannie Porter's Sporting House 166

Fargo 140
faro 131-132, 146
Federal cavalry 65
Federal cavalryman **63**
female outlaws 166
firewater 160
Fischer, Vardis 158
Fitzgerald, Jimmy 145
Florida cowhunter 12
Flynn, Errol 222, 228
Fonda, Henry 224, 228
Fonda, Jane 228
Ford, Bob 189
Ford, Charlie 107
Ford, John 180, 222, 223
Ford, Robert 107
Fort Abraham Lincoln 67
Fort Apache Stockade 240
Fort Bayard 70
Fort Clark 68
Fort Meade 72
Fort Sill 75
Fort Smith 80-95, **80**, **86**, 94
Fort Smith's Courtroom **86**, **90**, 163
Fort Worth and Denver City Railroad 18
Forty-niners 150, 162
Frank and Jesse 95
fringed hide gloves **22**
Frizzel, Lodisa 170
Froman, George 168

G
gamblers 144
Garner, James 228, 235, 237, 246
Garrett, Sheriff Pat 109, 111, 240
Gauchos 13
general store 196
Geronimo 70
Gettysburg 62
Gilded Age 178
Gish, Lillian 222
Glideen, Frederick Dilley 217
Glidden, Joseph F. 18
gold 152, 154
Gold Rush 154, 168
The Gold Rush 154
Gold Rushes and Mining Camps in the Early American West 158
Gold Rush widows 169
Golden, Johnny 148
Golden West 154
The Good, the Bad and the Ugly 230

Goodnight, Charles 17, **18**
Goodnight Loving Trail 17, 18
Governor Stanford Locomotive **184**
Grande, Joe 134
Grant, President 66, 85
Great Divide Basin 178
Great Migration 168
Great Plains 46
Great Revival 138
The Great Train Robbery 222
Great Western Cattle Trail 17
Greene, Lorne 235, 236
Grey, Zane 216, 218, 224
Grierson, Benjamin Henry 74
Gunsmoke 236
Guthrie, A.B. "Bud" 216, 217

H
half-dime novel **214**
Haji Mansei Toy Company 251
Hancock Homestead **168**
Hang 'Em High 95
Hansen, Rob 234
Harper's Weekly 138
Harris, W.H. 101
Harrison, President Benjamin 206
Hart, Pearl 166
Hart, William 228
Harte, Bret 154
Hauser, John 57
Hatch, Colonel Edward 74
Heiser **26**
"Hell on the Border" 91
Hell on Wheels 180
Hell's Half Acre 210
Henry rifle **23**
Hickok, Wild Bill 112, 142, 146, 189
The High Chaparral 236
High Noon 140, **231**
Hines, Reverend Gustavus 139
Hoffman, Lee 218
Holliday, Alice Jane 101
Holliday, Henry Burroughs 101
Holliday, John "Doc" **101**, 167, 189, 230
Hollow Horn Bear **52**
Holmes, Opal Laurel 158
Homestead Act 172
homesteaders 203
Hopalong Cassidy **215**
How the West Was Won 185
The Howdy Doody Show 240
huasos 13
Hubley 241, 243, 244, 246,

249
Hubley Colt 45, 247

I

Indian Breakfast **43**
Indian Removal Act 1830 47
Indian Territory 66
Indian Wars 68, 70, 73, 82
Ingalls, Laura (Wilder) 173, 190, 236
The Iron Horse 180
Iron Tail 57
Ivers, Poker Alice 149, 168

J

J. Muellers Shop 192
Jackson, President Andrew 47
James Gang 105, 106
James, Jesse Woodson 105, 105, 107, 111, 215
James, Robert 105
Jerky **42**, 42
John Deere chuck wagon 32
Johnson County War 215
Johnson, Dorothy Marie 218
Johnson, Terry C. 219
Judah, Theodore D. 178
Judge Parker's courtroom **86**
Judge Parker's gallows **88**

K

Kansas Pacific Railway **14**
Kelley's Saloon "The Bijou" **159**
Kennedy, Burt 228
Kenton 241, 245
Keogh, Captain 78
Kelton, Elmer 217
Keno House Brothel 164
Kilgore 249
Kiowa 68, 72
Kotsoteka Comanches 70
Kurosawa, Akira 228

L

L'Amour, Louis 35, 190, 215, 217, 218, 219, 220, 236
Ladd, Alan 228
La Pointe, Jenny 56
Lakota Sioux 58
Landon, Michael 236
lariat **23**
The Last of the Mohicans 215
Lazy Corn Fritters 38
Lee, Ang 234

Lee, Robert E. 65
Leffingwell, Thomas 212
Leonard, Elmore 217
Leone, Sergio 228, 234
Letters of a Woman Homesteader 173
Levi jeans **23**
Lincoln, President Abraham 178
Lincoln County Wars 109
"the line" 162
Little Crow 52
Little House on the Prairie 173
log homes **198-199, 202**
The Lone Ranger 235
Lone Star 241
Lonesome Dove 95
Louisville, Kentucky 70
Loving, Oliver 17
Lucretia 184
Lyle, John T. 17

M

Madams 162
"Madonnas of the Frontier" 173
The Magnificent Seven 232
Majors, Alexander 143
Maledon, George **88**
Mammoth 249
Mammy Pleasant 164
Mann, Anthony 224
Marcus, Josephine 101
Marrow, "Prairie Dog" Dave 101
Marsh, Mae 222
Martin, Dean 223, 229
Marvin, Lee 228
Marx, Louis 241
Marx Toy Company 240, 241, 245
Masterson, William Barclay (Bat) 100, 111, 147, **150**
Mattel 247, 248
Mature, Victor 222
Maverick 237
Maxwell House 108
Maxwell, Pete 111
McConnio, Preacher Garner 140
McCoy, Joseph G. 13
McDoulet, "Cattle" Annie **166**
McLain, Frank 101
McLure, Doug 235
McMurty, Larry 218
McQueen, Steve 228, 232, 245
Medicine Lodge Citizens' Posse 114

Mexican sombrero 21
Michigan Cavalry (7th) **63**
Miles, General Nelson A. 70
Milton Bradley 241
Miner **152**
Miniconjou Sioux 72
Mint Gambling Saloon 149
Miss Laura Smith's Brothel 163
Mississippi River boat **144**
Missouri-Style Barbequed Ribs 42
Mitchum, Robert 224
Mix, Tom 222, 224
Montana 164
Moore, Clayton 235
Morgan, Rose 166
Mormons 154, 168
Morricone, Ennio 228
mountain men 134, 135
"movers" 169
Mulford, Clarence E. 215, 234
Mulhall, Lucile 164
Mulhall, Colonel Zack 104

N

Native Americans 43-53
Native American artefacts 54-59
Native American winter camp **49**, 153
Navajo 51
Navajo mother **51**
Navajo war captain 51
The New Frontier 224
Newcomb, George "Bittercreek" 112
Nez Perce 79
Nichols 247
Nichols Stallion .45 Mark 2 revolver 247
Noir Westerns 223
Nylint 241
"nymphs du prairie"162

O

O.K. Corral 101
Oakley, Annie 56, 165
Occum, Reverend Samson 138
Oglala Sioux 57
Ohio Cavalry (5th) **65**
Ojibwa 57
Oklahoma City 211
Oklahoma District 211
"Oklahoma's Yodelling Cowboy" 229

Old Homestead 163
Old Lady Horse 184
Olinger, Robert 109, 111
Oregon Trail 136, 150
Orient Saloon 100, **146**
The "Outlaws" 106
Owens, Commodore Perry **99**, 100

P

Pacific Railroad Act 178
Pacific Railroad Convention 178
Paine, Lauran 217
"painted cats" 162
Paiute **12**
Pale Rider 140
Parker, Judge Isaac 80, 84, **85**, 87, 91, **94**
Parker, Cynthia Ann 49
Parker, Quanah **44-45**
Parker, Tomasa **44-45**
Parkhurst, Charlie 166
Parkman, Francis 136
parlor girl **162**
parlor houses 162
Peach Cobbler 40
Peckinpah, Sam 228
Pennsylvania Campaign 65
penny dreadfuls 214
Perkins, Anthony 228
Perry, Oklahoma **208, 209**
Peterson, Martin 139
Petillon, W.F. 101
Philadelphia Light Horse **62**
Phineas Banning's Stage Line 100
Pickford, Mary 222
Pikes Peake Express Company 140
Pinkerton Detective Agency 106
Pioneer Women 168
Pitt, Brad 234
Pleasant Valley War 99
Polk, President James 149
Pommel slicker 22
Pony Express 140, 142, 178
Porter, Lavinia 169
Poteau River 82
Powder Ridge Expedition 184
Powers, Bill 111
Prairie grass **203**
Prostitutes 164
Pryor brothers 17

Q

Quakers 168
Quahadi Comanches 70
quart **23**
Quatic 47
quilting 173

R

Randall, Josh 245
Rawhide 232
The Reconstruction 72
Red Cloud 52
Red Cloud's War 52, 185
Reed, Autie 67
Remington, Frederick 10, 215, 222
Remington rifle **69**
Remington single shot rifle **78**
Rendez vous 135
Rin Tin Tin Fort 240
Rio Lobo **228**
Rio Bravo 229
Ritter, Tex 223
Roberts, Pernell 235
Rodriguez, Robert 234
Rogers, John 82, **85**
Rogers, Mrs. John **84**
Rogers, Roy **212**, 223, 234, 235, 238, 242
Rogers, Will 20, **22**
Rogers' Historic Home **84, 85**
rodeo **29**
Roosevelt, President Theodore 211
Rose of Cimarron **167**
Ross, John 47
Ross, Reuben 138
Rough Hair 59
Round Valley Gunfight 99
Rowdy Yates 232
Rupp, Whitey 164
Russell, Kurt 230
Russell, William H. **142**
Russell's Central Overland 140
Ryan, Bud 103

S

saddle blanket 28
Samuel Dennison's Exchange 146
San Francisco 146, 150, 154, 178
Sand Creek Massacre 184
Santa Fe Railroad 184
"scarlet ladies" 162
Schaefer, Jack 216, 217

Schmidt, S.B. 181
Scott, Randolph 228
Selma 65
Selznick, David O. 223
Seminole 62
Seymour, Jane 236
Sharps carbine **65**
Sharps rifle **24**, 125
sheepskin-lined coat **22**
Sherman, General William Tecumseh 47, 66
Sherman Ranch, Kansas **16**
Shertinger, Victor 222
Shipman, David 212
Short, Luke 101, 147, **148**, 216
Short, Luke (novelist) 217
Sierra Nevada Mountains 152
Sinatra, Frank 140
Singing Grass 135
Sioux 51, 72
Sitting Bull **52, 53**
Slaughter, George W. 17
Slocum Westerns 220
Smith, Dave 91
Smith, Soapy 147
sod homestead **172**
sodbusters 190, 200, 201
"soiled doves" 158, 162
Southwestern Hotel **16**
Spearman, Frank Hamilton 215
Spencer guns 126
Spencer carbine Model 1865 **68**
Spider Gang 99
"sporting women" 162
Spotted Pup Dessert 39
Spotted Tail 47
Springfield guns 127
Springfield carbine stand **68**
Springfield Model 1873 **68**
spurs **21**
stagecoach **171**
Starr, Belle **94**, 95
Starr, Charles 145
Starr, Pearl **94**, 91
Stephens, Ann Sophia 214
Stetson **21**
Stevens, George 228
Stevens, Jeannie "Little Britches" 166
Stewart, Elinore Pruitt 173
Stewart, Jimmy 228, 230
"stickers" 169
Strauss, Levi 154
Street and Smith 215
Stuart Manufacturing Company 241

Sturges, John 228
Sun River Montana 168
Sutter, John 149
Sutter's Mill 149
Svee, Gary 219

T

Tales of the Argonauts 154
Taliaferro, Hardin E. 140
Taylor, John 139
Texas Brazos River Territory 104
Texas Camp Bread 37
Texas Longhorn 10
Texas Rangers **186**, 103
There Will be Blood 140
Timberline **161**
Tobacco Society 56
Tombstone 100, 101
Trail of Tears 82
Train, George Francis 174
Transcontinental Railway 174-185
True Grit 95
Tunstall, John 109
Twain, Mark 140, 181

U

Union Cavalryman **60**
Union Pacific 166, 179, 180, 181
Unique Art Manufacturing Company 251
US Cavalry 60-79
  4th 68
  5th **66**
  6th **70**
US Cavalry uniform **76**, 76-77
US Cavalry officer's uniform **77**
US Colored Cavalry **72**
US Land Office **208**
United States Marshals Service 87
Utah 158

V

Vaquero **10**, 13
Van Cleef, Lee 228
Vidor, King 223
Vinita, Oklahoma 87
Virginia Light Horse 62
Virginia Quarter-Miler 24
The Virginian (novel) 214
The Virginian (film) 224

W

W. H. McCoy's claim 209
Wallace, Governor 109
Walsh, Raoul 224
Wayne, John 223, 224, 228, 230#
Weaver, Dennis 236
Webner, Frank E. **142**
Wells Fargo 99, 143
Western cowboy saddles **25**
Western fiction 212-237
Western movies 220-223
Western shotguns 128-129
Western towns 186
Western toys 238
Western Union **194**
Whispering Smith 216
Whitman, Walt 156, 174
Wichita, Kansas 189
Wild Bill Hickok 113, 147, 148, 236
The Wild Bunch 166, 167
Wild West Hotel **208**
Wilder, Gene 228
Williams, Mike 113
Williamsburg 62
Winchester rifles 120-124
Winchester 1866 carbine
Winchester Model 1866 **24**
Winchester rifles **114**
Winchester Trapper carbine **74**
Wister, Owen 215, 222
Women in the West 156
Wounded Knee Massacre 57, 66
Wyeth, N.C. 107, 113, 147
Wyandotte 241
Wyler, William 224

Y

Yankiboy 241
Yellow Train 65

Z

Zinnemann, Fred 228

Acknowledgments

J.P. Bell, Fort Smith, Arkansas

Johnny C. Brumley, Texas

The Buffalo Bill Historical Center, Cody Wyoming

Judy Crandall, Eagle Editions, Hamilton, Montana

Colorado History Society

Peter Greenhalf and the Hastings Museum & Art Gallery

Walter Harder, Kamloops Secondary School, British Columbia.

Patrick F. Hogan, Rock Island Auction Co., Moline, Illinois

Stuart Holman, Auctioneer, Cincinnati, Ohio

Andrew Howick, MPTV, Van Nuys, California

Kansas City Historical Society

Robert G. McCubbin, El Paso, Texas

Tom McLeod, Museum of the Pacific, Texarkana, Texas

Jerzy Miller, Lazy C.J. Cattle Co, Texas

Donna Morgan, Director, Callaway Family Association, Texas

Emily Lovick, Fort Smith National Historic Site, Fort Smith, Arkansas

The National Archives

Kathy Weiser, Legends of America, Lenexa, Kansas